The
Real Estate Agent's
Business Planner

The
Real Estate Agent's
Business Planner

Practical Strategies for Maximizing
Your Success

Bridget McCrea

American Management Association

New York • Atlanta • Brussels • Chicago • Mexico City • San Francisco
Shanghai • Tokyo • Toronto • Washington, D.C.

Library of Congress Cataloging-in-Publication Data

McCrea, Bridget.
        The real estate agent's business planner : practical strategies for
    maximizing your success / Bridget McCrea.
            p.   cm.
        Includes bibliographical references and index.
        ISBN 0-8144-0846-X (pbk.)
        1. Real estate business—Planning.   2. Real estate agents.   I. Title.

    HD1375.M368   2005
    333.33'068'4—dc22   2005001184

Printing number

10   9   8   7   6   5   4   3   2   1

Contents

Foreword

"FOREWARNED, FOREARMED;

TO BE PREPARED IS HALF THE VICTORY."

—MIGUEL DE CERVANTES SAAVEDRA

Very few people actually enjoy the planning process. Most would rather jump in feetfirst and let the chips fall where they may, never taking the time to actually map out a viable plan of action for success.

As someone who works often with new and existing real estate agents, I can tell you that they're no different. In fact, there's almost a built-in resistance that comes up as soon as you mention the word *planning*—as if doing so would somehow take away from the person's ability to succeed.

To make the task more digestible, I boil planning down to two key factors: effort and accountability. On one hand, planning involves mapping out the actual effort put forth during the workday. On the other, it helps you be more accountable for your options, providing valuable benchmarks on which to measure future actions.

Since most brokers would rather see agents making their way to the closing table than spending their time preparing for the next twelve months, those real estate leaders generally don't push planning as an important component of success. As a result, few agents grasp the basics of planning, nor do they ever realize how vital forecasting can be in an industry where they operate as small-business owners, not employees.

Successful planning starts with a hard look at your own personal finances, particularly if you're a newer agent who needs to get through those first six to twelve months without a paycheck. Using a spreadsheet in Microsoft Excel or another type of cash flow system, you gain a clear picture of where you are financially as an agent, where you're headed, and exactly what you need to do to get there.

This book will show you how to create a solid business plan. Whether you're new to the business or an experienced agent who is looking to increase sales and profits, a plan will assist you in managing cash flow in an environment where commission checks are neither predictable nor uniform. Having a plan will help you work through those ebbs and flows, and especially prevent you from going into panic mode when you realize that it could be two months before you receive your next check.

Projections are an important component of any plan. Real-life pressures such as auto repair, loss of a spouse's job, or deals that fall through can wreak havoc on any business owner—particularly the one who has never mapped out a plan for success. If you don't want closing the doors to be your only option, you'll want to take the time to assess your finances, create a plan, develop a marketing strategy, flesh out your objectives, factor in necessities like taxes and insurance, and generate longer-term goals for your future.

Knowing that real estate agents are their bread and butter, today's brokers have instituted rigorous new-agent training programs that cover everything from how to create comparative market analyses and fill out contracts, to the best way to handle listing appointments and negotiations. Still, many agents get into the business with stars in their eyes. Those stars keep twinkling when they hear talk about agents making money hand over fist in this time of high property appreciation and rising home sales, and they want a piece of the action.

With its low barriers to entry, the real estate industry beckons with welcome arms but does not stress the importance of good planning. It's an easy requirement to overlook. Instead, the business focuses on the grand prize: the new agents' dream of that all-important first commission check.

"Those agents who achieve success early in their careers," says Lori Arnold, president of a Dallas-based Coldwell Banker franchise, "are the ones with the most detailed business plans." By that she means planning how you're going to feed yourself during the first few lean months, budgeting for association dues as soon as you hang your license with a broker, and finding creative ways to market yourself without breaking the bank. Also of importance is acting and operating like a small-business owner, and learning how to manage a fluctuating income that, without proper planning, can find you living large one month, and completely broke the next.

This book was written for both new agents coming into the business as well as existing agents who need assistance getting these and other planning issues on track. Maybe you got into the business and did well for a while, only to find your business now stagnating for no apparent reason. With no plan in place, and no means of reviewing specific performance measurements, how will you know what steps to take to get your business growing again?

The answers are in the pages of this book. It was written for all agents but specifically those who have their eye on success and would like a roadmap to help get them there. I hope it serves you well.

David Fletcher, President, Agents Boot Camp

Acknowledgments

I'd like to thank my editors at AMACOM Books for helping make my real estate books a reality, as well as the many experts, trade organizations, and real estate professionals who were kind enough to lend their time and expertise to help make this book a reality. I extend a special thank you to my family for their support, and for helping with the research, editing, and legwork that went into creating this comprehensive planning guide for real estate agents.

The
Real Estate Agent's
Business Planner

CHAPTER ONE

Taking Stock

''ALL THE FLOWERS OF
ALL THE TOMORROWS ARE
IN THE SEEDS OF TODAY AND YESTERDAY.''

—ANONYMOUS

Before you got into real estate, you probably had some very valid reasons for doing so. It could have been the promises of a great income, the flexible schedule that would allow you to set your own hours, the chance to work with people in your community, or the desire to learn more about the intricacies of the real estate industry. Maybe a family member was in the business, or maybe the For Sale signs scattered around your neighborhood prompted you to look for a way to take advantage of the real estate boom.

Whatever the motivation, you most likely took a short real estate course, sat for your salesperson exam and—hopefully— became one of the roughly 45 percent of people who pass it the first time out. If not, you probably took it again and passed, then hung your license at a local brokerage that met your criteria.

From that point on, your new career has probably felt a lot like a whirlwind: spending time in training classes, doing floor time, farming for clients in your neighborhood, using the Internet to develop leads, and spending weekends showing homes. You're probably tied to your cell phone, answering each call to make sure you don't miss any potential clients. You're running from one house to the next, hoping that somewhere along the way one of those contacts turns into a sale, which a few weeks later turns into money in your pocket.

Nowhere along the way did anyone make you sit down and take a very simple entrepreneurial quiz to make sure you're well suited for business ownership. Well, better late than never.

Here's a brief one to take right now. Answer yes or no to each of the following eleven questions:

1. Like most successful entrepreneurs, am I an optimist and a risk taker?
2. Do I have the self-starter determination to get this thing going and the discipline to keep it on track?
3. Do I work hard?
4. Can I take responsibility for my own actions?
5. Am I a good problem solver?
6. Am I organized?
7. Do I have the physical stamina to work long hours?
8. Am I willing to work weekends and evenings—the times when most home buyers will be out looking for homes?
9. Can I finance this business myself for at least six to twelve months?
10. Will my family be supportive of my entrepreneurial efforts?
11. Do I have the basic skills required to start and successfully run a business, or do I have access to a mentor who can help me through those critical early stages?

If you answered yes to more than half of the questions, consider yourself a good candidate for a real estate career. If you answered no to five or more questions, don't despair. You may simply need to change your approach to work, your mind-set, and your way of managing tasks, challenges, and problems. Although no one can instill physical stamina, and pessimists have a hard time seeing the glass as half-full, there are always experienced mentors, colleagues, and college courses to turn to for education on the fine points of running a small business. Combine those resources with a great business plan and you just may surprise yourself . . . and your family and friends.

Despite the critical importance of a business plan, many entrepreneurs drag their feet when it comes to preparing a written document. They argue that their marketplace changes too fast for a business plan to be useful or that they just don't have enough time. But just as a builder won't begin construction without a blueprint, eager business owners shouldn't rush into new ventures without a business plan. Before you begin writing your business plan, ask yourself these four questions:

1. What service or product does your business provide and what needs does it fill?
2. Who are the potential customers for your product or service, and why will they purchase it from you?
3. How will you reach your potential customers?
4. Where will you get the financial resources to start your business?

As fundamental as they may seem, these four core components are critical to your business success—whether that venture is a hair salon, bookstore, or an individual real estate agent who sells homes. Know your service, your customers, how to reach them, and what resources you'll need to get there, and you'll soon find yourself on the path to success.

The Whirlwind

Caught up in the whirlwind that is your new real estate career, have you stopped to do any of the following?

❏ Create a business plan that outlines your professional goals, aspirations, expectations, and financial needs.

❏ Open a business bank account in order to keep personal and business income and expenses separate.

❏ Set up a spreadsheet or other mechanism for tracking your work performance and resultant financial rewards.

❏ Develop an effective plan for marketing yourself to your potential clients.

❏ Map out a plan for living comfortably on a fluctuating, unpredictable income.

❏ After you figure out who your ideal client is, decide on the best approach for reaching out to that person.

❏ Think about how you're going to purchase your own health and life insurance.

❏ Decide how you'll handle long-term financial goals, such as retirement plans.

❏ Select a business entity, such as a sole proprietorship, corporation, or partnership, that best suits your business.

❏ Factor in issues like tax planning and preparation, since you're now an independent contractor.

❏ Create an action plan for personal and professional development.

If you answered no to even one of these eleven statements, you'll want to take a step back and create an action plan for your business that encompasses these and other key matters. The exercise works for new and existing agents alike. For new licensees, the step probably won't have to be too big, since you're either just getting started or only a few months into it.

Existing agents may have to stretch themselves a bit further, since they've already tasted some level of success and may not see the value in a formal business planning process. For new agents, it's important to remember that it's never too late to kick off a good planning process based on what you've already achieved and your own future aspirations in the industry.

We'll call this exercise "Taking Stock." See Worksheet 1-1, which you can use to answer some key questions about yourself and your career.

WORKSHEET 1-1: TAKING STOCK

1. Why did I get into the real estate business in the first place? (Were the motives financial in nature, were you looking for a new career, did you want to get out and interact with customers on a daily basis?)

_____

_____

_____

_____

2. What steps have I taken so far in my career to achieve this early goal?

_____

_____

_____

_____

3. Have I created a mission statement for my business? A good mission statement can be a foundation for assessing needs, determining objectives, setting goals, and making the daily decisions that will help you achieve success as an agent. If not, start crafting one here by answering these questions: Who am I? What am I trying to accomplish? What do I value?

_____

_____

_____

_____

4. How do I measure success in the industry, and what specific steps do I need to take to reach that level of success in real estate?

_____

_____

_____

_____

5. How successful have I been so far in the business, and am I taking the steps outlined in questions 1–4 to achieve my goals? Or, have I skipped steps along the way, thus lessening my chances to reach my success goals?

_____

_____

_____

6. What type of marketing plan do I have in place, and does it include marketing efforts that are cohesive and productive?

_____

_____

_____

7. Am I acting like a small-business owner, even though I'm working for a broker? What steps have I taken so far that prove this, and what could I be doing better in this regard?

_____

_____

_____

8. Where do I stand financially right now? What level of cash reserves do I have to cover my business and personal expenses for the next six to twelve months while I build my business?

_____

_____

_____

9. In what ways do other people in my life (such as a spouse and/ or children) rely on me financially? If there are no such individuals in my life, does that mean I have the luxury of spending the next few months building my business without having to worry about earning a significant level of commissions?

_____

_____

_____

10. Do I have health insurance coverage for my family and myself? Do I have life insurance coverage (particularly important if you are the primary wage earner in the family)? If not, do I—as an independent contractor—have the means of getting either or both of these coverages?

_____

_____

_____

11. How will I plan the next few years of my personal and work life, factoring in issues like my children's college education, long-term care for elderly relatives, and retirement for myself?

_____

_____

_____

Once you've made mental notes or jotted down answers to the questions in Worksheet 1-1, you'll also want to take some time to assess your answers and use them to help ascertain:

- ❏ Where you stand right now
- ❏ Where you want to be professionally in the next six to twelve months
- ❏ Where you want to be, both professionally and personally, in five to ten years

Your answers to the first two questions will give you a good foundation to work with, even if you haven't yet laid that groundwork. Take the time to figure out the "whys" of your career choice. It could have been as simple as a friend telling you how great you would be at it, and that's fine. Then, look at the steps you've taken so far—no matter how small—to turn that idea into a reality.

For those of you who got into real estate thinking that because you hang your license at a certain brokerage you're an employee of that company, questions three, six, and seven will be particularly telling. If you haven't yet developed a mission statement for your business, and if you still feel like an employee (even though you aren't punching a clock or earning a steady paycheck), then it's time to start acting like a small-business owner. It's also time to develop a marketing plan, since customers aren't (always) going to come to you. You'll want to incorporate time-tested efforts (farming neighborhoods for leads, asking for referrals, taking out ads in the Sunday paper) with newer concepts (using online lead-generation services and automatic property-listing alerts through your local Multiple Listing Service) to come up with an affordable, workable plan.

Questions four and five deal with success—a fairly nebulous concept, since everyone's idea of success is different. Is success in real estate characterized by the person who has been in the industry for twenty years, closes ten deals a month, drives a fancy car, and vacations every year on the French Riviera? Or is it the agent who works in the inner city, helping ten or twelve underserved families achieve the dream of home ownership every year? Figure out where you fit between these two extremes, and then come up with a basic idea of how you will achieve it.

The last four questions are particularly important, since most agents are left to their own devices to generate business, close deals, and earn commission checks—which aren't always regular, nor are they uniform in amount. Most brokers suggest agents come into the business with four to six months' cash reserves to cover their expenses in this initial phase of operation, but those same brokers usually stress the fact that it doesn't mean it's going to take six months to do business. I've heard of agents who closed deals during their first week in business, and others who took up to a year to get that first deal under their belt. A new agent's first sale is a milestone that most brokers and office managers put a lot of emphasis on, since the frustration that comes from closing that first transaction can drive agents out of the business in a year or less.

The questions about health and life insurance, college savings, and retirement are equally as important, since they will get you to think past your career and assess the overall life you want to live. Since real estate offices don't provide benefits, you'll want to check with your local and state business associations (the National Association of Realtors® has an affiliate that offers coverage to members in certain states, for example) or try purchasing it on your own, depending on where you're located and what your specific needs are. The same goes for life insurance and any other financial obligations that will need to be taken care of over the next five to ten years.

Laying It All Out

Once you've taken stock of your business and personal situation, you'll be able to start planning your success in an industry where competition is stiff and the rewards that come from hard work can be handsome and varied (ranging from monetary rewards to industry recognitions to the sheer feeling of accomplishment that comes from helping to close a difficult deal). This book is divided into eight sections, each of which will cover a key part of the planning process. Once you've worked your way through it, you'll have a good handle on the following planning components:

❏ *Basic Business Planning:* The elements of a good plan, developing financial projections for your first (and subsequent) years in the business, reviewing and revising your plan regularly, and where to go for help in developing a successful business plan.

❏ *Your Marketing Plan:* Developing a targeted marketing plan and sticking with it, finding and cultivating a niche, budgeting for maximum effectiveness, measuring results, and using that information to tweak your plan.

❏ *Setting Goals and Objectives:* Creating attainable goals and objectives, updating those elements regularly, assessing your own needs (both personal and professional), and using that information to set the kind of goals that will help you get ahead in the field.

❏ *Managing a Fluctuating Income:* Taking steps that will help even out the fluctuations, dealing with them in an effective manner when the checks do ebb and flow, and creating budgets that ensure your long-term financial success in the industry.

❏ *Tax Planning:* Budgeting for taxes, making estimated tax payments, finding a good accountant to handle your tax preparation and year-round planning, and working with a financial planner on longer-term tax-planning issues.

❏ *Personal and Professional Development:* Learning to prioritize, enriching yourself through continuing education and certifications, supporting and growing your business, creating an overall sales strategy for your business, knowing when to hire help or form a team, and running a business that is not only financially rewarding, but also enjoyable and fulfilling.

❏ *Acting Like a Business Owner:* Setting up your business structure, creating a different set of books and bank accounts for your company, paying yourself a paycheck (rather than just dumping commission checks into your personal account), and the value of creating banking relationships and joining trade organizations.

❏ *Planning for the Long-Term:* Developing a big picture view of your career and finances, taking care of important issues like health and life insurance, saving for retirement and college savings, and planning not only for your next big sale, but also the next ten to twenty years of your life.

At this point, you may be asking yourself: Isn't this an awful lot of planning? The answer is yes, it is, but the good news is that this book will help you break down the process into manageable chunks. It's designed to hit the areas of highest to least priority for the typical agent, although not everyone will approach the planning process in the same fashion. For example, a single mother who just got licensed could be more concerned about managing a fluctuating income, and a married agent who is just starting a family might be more concerned about being able to establish a college fund for his first child.

To get the most out of your planning, you'll want to follow these basic guidelines:

❑ *Start at square one:* Begin with some business planning basics and outline your overall plan first before going back and beefing up areas of most concern for your particular situation.

❑ *Do your homework:* Put some time into researching your market, your potential customers, and your own financial situation to come up with a realistic picture of where you are right now, where you want to be, and how you're going to get there.

❑ *Write it down:* Don't try to commit this one to memory. Jot down notes as you think through your situation and your future goals and dreams, then use those notes to create a written business plan.

❑ *Network, but do your own thing:* You can learn a lot from existing agents, but no one agent's plan is going to be right for another. As you pick the brains of those around you for ideas, cull those that sound like they would be most applicable to you and discard the rest. Then, use the best of the best to develop your own plan.

❑ *Update regularly:* Like life, a business plan is a work in progress. You'll want to review your overall plan at least yearly, if not on a quarterly basis, to make sure you're on track. If you've met your goals, revise them. If you're much further off than you thought you would be, you may want to make the goals more attainable and tangible.

❑ *Make the time for it:* The beauty of small-business planning is that it costs little more than time. And although it's true that new agents are usually time strapped trying to start their careers, find customers, and make money, it will pay to go through this early planning exercise before you get too far into it. The same goes for the existing agent who has never taken the time to plan.

Finding Value

In many cases, the planning process itself can be more valuable than the resultant paper- or computer-based documents that are churned out. Preparing a sound business plan requires time and effort, but the benefits greatly exceed the costs. Building the plan forces a potential entrepreneur to look at her business idea in the harsh light of reality, and requires the owner to assess the company's chances of success more objectively.

"The real value in preparing a business plan is not so much in the plan itself as it is in the process the entrepreneur goes through to create the plan," says one professor of entrepreneurship at a large U.S. college. "Although the finished product is useful, the process of building a plan requires an entrepreneur to subject his idea to an objective, critical evaluation. What he learns about his company, its target market, its financial requirements, and other factors can be essential to his success."

Unfortunately, most businesspeople don't see the value of taking the time to work through the planning process. Real estate agents are notorious for breezing through their educational courses, zipping through their exam, loading up on business cards, and hitting the street to try to make some money. Some have certainly succeeded with this gung-ho attitude, but many more find themselves bogged down by the complexities of doing business. Instead of stopping to take a breath, they plod along, hoping for success.

Others do take the time to plan, but they use ineffective

DOWN TO BASICS

You don't need a course to get started on your own business plan. Just be sure you include the following:

❏ *Budget:* Start with a basic personal budget so you know what you need to survive during your first year or two in business. Then, plan a separate business budget that ties in with your own finances, since the two will probably be intertwined during your start-up phase. Most important, be honest and realistic and gain a clear understanding of your own monthly financial needs for your first year.

❏ *Set Goals:* This is a key step for new agents, who must know their goals if they expect to be able to meet them. A few concrete goals that you can set as an agent are:

I plan to have my interviews completed by

_____.

I plan to have my license placed by _____.

Therefore I should have my first commission check by _____.

Which means I should have my first sale by _____.

❏ *Form a Support Team:* This team should be made up of your broker (for marketing tools, office space, and training), a mortgage lender (who can prequalify your prospects, take buyers' applications, and order appraisals), and a title company (to conduct title searches, order termite inspections, and prepare closing documents). "Your support team is vital to your success," says David Fletcher, president of Agents Boot Camp. "It will help you in more ways than you can imagine when prospects are hard to qualify for a mortgage or the closing starts falling apart."

❏ *Learn the Real Estate Lingo:* The sooner you learn how to talk the talk in real estate, the better off you will be. A few key words surrounding *floor time*, for example, include:

Closed Floor—All calls go to the listing agent. Agents sometimes are paged and have a certain amount of time to call back. It they do not call back, the call goes to the floor agent.

Open Floor—An open floor usually means you can get floor time as soon as you are familiar with the phone system and can work with prospects. Another important real estate term is *farming*, or working in a specific area (subdivision, zip code, etc.) consistently to develop listing and sales leads.

strategies for doing so. Simply purchasing a $49 business planning software program and answering all of the questions that it throws at you doesn't guarantee that you'll end up with a good plan. Although such programs can help you get your ducks lined up and your brain in planning mode, it takes more than just a computer program to create a plan for real estate success. In fact, it's more important that you have spent enough time planning than it is to have it in a nifty computer program or package.

The Real Deal

For any plan to be effective, it must incorporate not only your work life, but also your family life and your personal goals and dreams. Notorious for working around the clock, seven days a week, real estate agents are particularly prone to getting caught up in the all-work-and-no-play way of life. Avoiding this vicious cycle can be as simple as scheduling your kid's soccer games in your Palm Pilot, just as you would an appointment, or hiring a part-time secretary to field e-mail messages that come through your Web site.

As you embark on your real estate career (or put your efforts into growing your existing business), such suggestions may seem trivial, but they are important. Most real estate agents are doers. They're quick to volunteer, get involved with their communities, and even run for public office. They help out at their children's schools, assist home buyers during the moving process, and do errands for them when needed. Too often, they turn into overdoers because they've never taken the time to plan. As a result, they miss a few critical areas of the business start-up process, like:

❏ Collecting critical market information that will lead to competitive advantages, lucrative niches, and the ability to tap market trends that their competitors may be unaware of

❏ Focusing their activities to make the best of materials and resources (such as technology tools)

❏ Understanding the industry as a whole and how it operates, which in turn enhances their ability to anticipate and deal with business challenges as they crop up

❏ Gaining introspection about goals and aspirations, both personal and professional

Of course, many agents cruise along in the industry without much planning. Usually these folks have a large network of friends, family, and colleagues to keep their pipelines full. They may also have family members who have been in the business, shown them the ropes, and pointed business in their direction. The rest of the agents who are competing for business in the real world, however, would achieve much faster and more efficiently if they had a plan of action in place before getting in too deep.

The good news is that planning doesn't have to be expensive or time-consuming. The better news is that any amount of time or money that you put into it is sure to pay off tenfold. Darla Scott of ManagementMaster in Philadelphia says most sales associates in the real estate industry fail because of a lack of written objectives, a lack of structure and self-discipline in their daily activities, and a lack of ongoing training and support.

Scott should know. She has a recognized twenty-seven-year track record of success that has involved all aspects of real estate operations, including incentive-based compensation design, relocation, recruiting, marketing, postmerger reorganization, and branch, regional, and title-company management. "Real estate is a self-driven business," says Scott. "An agent must develop a KISS (keep it simple, stupid) business plan and relentlessly stick to it."

For agents, keeping it simple means committing a few key tenets to memory. Here are a few to start with, though you may have a few of your own to add to the list:

- ❏ Treat your real estate career as a business.
- ❏ Create a successful business plan and a budget, then live by them.
- ❏ Tweak those plans as needed, to adjust to changes in your business or life.
- ❏ Realize that you have to spend money to make money, and don't be afraid to invest a little in a gadget or resource that will help you generate new or manage existing business.
- ❏ Pinpoint a salary level that you need to achieve, then work backward to figure out how many sales you need to meet that income requirement.
- ❏ Separate work and play. It's not always easy to do in real estate with a cell phone attached to your hip, but take an intentional day or two off every week—just like you would in a nine-to-five job.
- ❏ Be realistic about your real estate career. Realize that it could be a few years before you can afford the luxury foreign car or the waterfront home that the more experienced agent flaunts at the office.
- ❏ Don't be discouraged by small setbacks; instead, chalk them up to experience and use that knowledge on future business dealings.

With this book, you'll be able to do all of this and more, and you'll learn some business planning fundamentals in these pages to determine the best format for your own plan.

Once you've answered the various questions and taken the quizzes in chapter 2, you'll find that your personal and professional picture will be much more focused. You'll also have at your fingertips the basic information necessary to create a business plan that will help you shape the future of your business. Are you ready to get started? Great, now just turn the page.

CHAPTER TWO

Business Planning 101

''THE WISE MAN BRIDGES

THE GAP BY LAYING OUT THE PATH

BY MEANS OF WHICH HE CAN GET

FROM WHERE HE IS TO WHERE HE WANTS TO GO.''

—JOHN PIERPONT MORGAN

Most new agents are afraid of the amount of time they'll have to take to create a written business plan, but those who do spend the time—and the experts who advocate this step—agree that the payoff is well worth it.

"A business plan really helps the agent focus," says Lori Arnold, president at Dallas-based Coldwell Banker Apex, Realtors®. "It's easy to get pulled in many directions in this business, and having a solid plan helps both the new and the experienced agent concentrate on what they need to tackle on a daily basis in order to make their income."

Of the many new and experienced agents that Coldwell Banker Apex hires annually, Arnold estimates that 75 percent lack a solid business plan. Ignoring this step trips up all agents but can be particularly harmful to the new agent who doesn't factor in costs like business cards and MLS dues, and winds up in the hole financially before her first commission check is cut.

The good news is that getting started with a business plan is simple enough. All it takes is a first draft to break through the writer's block, and it can be something scribbled on the proverbial cocktail napkin. When it's time to take this step, look first at these four important areas:

1. A description of your business and business activities.
2. A brief outline of your marketing plan (see chapter 3 for more in-depth discussion on creating a marketing plan).
3. The financing details: How will you finance your business, and what will that initial investment cover?

4. The management aspect: How will you manage your business through its first six to twelve months of life?

Before You Start Writing Your Business Plan

Let's face it, writing down notes about your new venture, deciding how you'll get out into the community to reach consumers, and managing your company (which will probably consist of simply managing yourself) isn't where most agents get tripped up during their first few months in the business. Because of a lack of personal funds when they get into the business, financing is where they run into the most stumbling blocks. Financial obligations that come up while they're in the learning stages can make a bad situation worse, and often drive agents back to hourly jobs and steady paychecks.

With that in mind, we're going to concentrate on the dollars and cents of the real estate business first because your finances should determine the rest of the plan. We will help you create a complete business plan later in the book. You don't want to find yourself staring at an empty bank balance when you're just thirty days away from your first commission check, so take the early steps necessary to make sure that doesn't happen. According to estimates, nine out of ten real estate agents leave the business within their first five years, mainly because of the time it takes to earn a respectable living.

Experience Pays

If you're wondering just what a "respectable living" is for a real estate agent, the National Association of Realtors reported the following median gross, pretax incomes for agents in 2002, based on their number of years on the job:

Less than 5 years: $35,400
6 to 10 years: $49,500
11 to 15 years: $58,700
16 to 25 years: $64,900
26 years or more: $67,500

To make sure he didn't wind up being one of the majority of agents who throw in the towel before getting a taste of success, one agent took an honest look at his own financial picture and decided how to finance both his new real estate career and lifestyle during the start-up phase of his new business.

In need of help, he signed up for a local company's Basic Training course. From it, he took away a range of valuable strategies and tools to use in the field. He considers one of the most important to be the "Survival Business Plan" spreadsheet, on which he was able to map out his entire financial year prior to picking up the phone to call his first client.

"It was a real eye-opener for me," says the agent. "It showed me how to plan for success in this business." He started by filling in an entire year's worth of data on his personal and family finances and liabilities (mortgage payments, food expenses, etc.) as well as business expenses (association dues, training costs, etc.). The exercise showed him in exactly what time frame he needed to make his first sale, how long his personal or family reserves would last, how much positive cash flow he would have by the end of his first year in the business, plus other valuable insights.

Because this agent analyzed his own finances and capabilities before going into real estate on a full-time basis, he gained a clear view of exactly what needs to be done not only to survive, but also to thrive in the competitive real estate business. During his first six months in the business he closed three transactions and was already working on five active listings. He broke even during that first year and was on track for a 20 to 25 percent gain in profits during his second year in the business.

"I used a very realistic, spreadsheet-based plan that showed me exactly where I was at financially, where I needed to be in six months, and what I needed to do to get there," says the agent. "I know that I need to list a certain number of homes and complete a specific number of sales per month to reach my goals, and that's exactly what I'm doing."

The Survival Business Plan that this agent uses is the brainchild of David R. Fletcher, president of Agents Boot Camp (www.agentsbootcamp.com). A twenty-five-year real estate veteran, Fletcher owned an independent real estate company for twelve years and was senior vice president of a large franchise for six years. These days he helps newly licensed agents who have no direct sales or prospecting experience, as well as independent broker/owners who need to compete with the franchises that have a professional training system.

For them, Fletcher conducts monthly Boot Camp seminars that open agents' and brokers' eyes to the "financial, economic, and sales realities of the real estate business." He does it through seminars entitled Survival Selling, Survival Listing, Survival Listing Presentations, and Survival Goal Setting. For new agents in particular, Fletcher drills in one crucial starting point: "Know and understand your finances before you get into the real estate business." That means knowing:

❏ How much cash you have in reserve
❏ How much money your spouse or significant other is making each month

❏ How much commission you can reasonably expect during your first six to twelve months in business

Those income numbers are then offset by expenses that include car insurance, car payments, mortgage payments, and homeowners insurance on the family side and marketing expenses, long-distance phone bills, and postage on the business side. From there, new agents can figure their monthly cash flow and determine how many closings, sales, and prospects they need to get each month to reach a positive cash flow.

"New agents really need to understand the financial implications of their undertaking, but most don't," says Fletcher. In fact, the National Association of Realtors (NAR) reports that 85 percent of new sales agents have no past sales experience, which means they don't know how to prospect, market, or sell either.

Because most new agents work solely on commissions, they must have at least some level of cash reserve saved *before* getting started. Realize that an agent's average annual income is about $35,400, and factor that into your projections to figure out whether you can afford to put all of your time into real estate.

To improve on those low income numbers, agents need to figure out their prospect-to-sales ratio and improve on it over time. To make that happen, real estate agents must get a handle on the following key aspects of their careers:

❏ Knowing their finances
❏ Learning how to sell
❏ Staying focused on their careers
❏ Not losing their vision for success
❏ Doing their homework
❏ Interviewing at least three real estate offices before choosing a broker

❏ Reading the broker's policy manual

❏ Thoroughly understanding the compensation setup (which varies from office to office)

❏ Sticking with their decision in a positive, focused manner

Agents will greatly increase their chances of succeeding in real estate by getting an early handle on their finances and using that information to make first-year projections and beyond.

"The problem is that too many agents are working under extreme financial pressure, which multiplies every other problem by at least ten times," says Fletcher. "But if an agent has the financial strength and a good solid plan there's no reason she shouldn't be extremely successful in the business within a two- to three-year period, depending on how hard and smart she works."

And although a business plan covers different aspects of running a business, the financial planning that an agent will have to go through during the process will by far be the most valuable part of the plan. Agents need to know how much reserve they need for the first six months to one year, plain and simple. The problem is that many new agents overlook expenses like Realtor® association dues and advertising costs when considering their start-up fees. A few extra hundred dollars per month for such expenses may not sound significant when you're sitting in real estate school, but such charges add up and can wreak havoc on agents who work months to achieve their first commission check.

Consider the sample budget in Table 2-1 on pages 32 and 33 and create a similar budget for your finances.

With these financials in mind, you'll be able to create a monthly cash flow and determine how many closings, sales, and prospects you need to get each month to reach a positive cash flow. By using tools like Excel spreadsheets that outline the financial factors mentioned above, agents can gain a foothold in the industry whether they have past sales experience or not.

Once a plan is in place, agents can also more effectively manage cash flow (instead of blowing an entire commission check within a day of receiving it) because they're innately aware of what expenses they need to cover, how much to keep for themselves, and how much to allocate for taxes. Without these solid numbers in mind, Fletcher says, an agent's dreams and aspirations can quickly dissolve into stressful, frustrating situations—particularly if the agent's significant other suffers a job loss, his home needs a new roof, or he wants to take a family vacation.

"There are real-life pressures associated with any commission-only jobs, and they have to be dealt with early, as opposed to later," says Fletcher. "Once an agent is out in the field, under pressure to perform, it will be hard to deal with issues like debt and financial woes. Sometimes the only option is to get out of the business and go back to a full-time, salaried, or hourly position."

Now that you have a clear picture of how much you need to survive, you next have to understand how the commissions work.

Figuring Your Commission

Before you start creating goals to make your minimum salary, you'll want to have a solid grasp on just how your commissions break down. Realize that a 3 percent commission (for either the buy or sell side of the transaction) on a $100,000 home doesn't necessarily equate to a $3,000 commission check. You must

Table 2-1. The Survival Business Plan.

MY BUSINESS PLAN (SAMPLE)

AGENT A owns her own business and has trouble setting goals. She needs a business plan that can show her what her goals must be to survive, where her most serious cash flow problems will occur, and at what point she will break even. She needs to know what her personal and business expenses will be and how it all adds up. What should her first year's goals be? How much can she expect to earn her first year? What about her business expenses? We have assumed a $1,500 commission on a $100,000 sale for purposes of this sample.

Month	1	2	3	4	5	6	7	8	9	10	11	12	Total
INCOME													
Spouse Income (after tax)	2,000	2,000	2,000	2,000	2,000	2,000	2,000	2,200	2,200	2,200	2,200	2,200	25,000
Agent A's Commission	2,250	1,500	2,000	1,500	1,500	1,500	2,250	2,250	1,800	2,250	2,250	2,250	23,300
Other													0
TOTAL INCOME	4,250	3,500	4,000	3,500	3,500	3,500	4,250	4,450	4,000	4,450	4,450	4,450	48,300
PERSONAL EXPENSES													
Car Ins. #1	150			150			150			150			600
Car Ins. #2									500				500
Car Payment #1	200	200	200	200	200	200	200	200	200	200	200	200	2,400
Car Payment #2	180	180	180	180	180	180	180	180					1,440
Car Repair					500					300			800
Charitable Contr.	100	100	100	100	100	100	100	100	100	100	100	100	1,200
Clothes	200	100	100	100	100	100	100	100	200	200	100	100	1,500
Education	200	100	100	100	100	100	200	100	100	100	100	100	1,400
Food	200	200	200	200	200	300	300	200	200	200	200	300	2,700
Gas	200	200	200	200	200	200	200	200	200	200	200	200	2,400
Health Insurance	150	150	300	150	150	300	150	150	300	150	150	300	2,400
Internet Related	50	50	50	50	50	50	50	50	50	50	50	50	600
Credit Cards	100	100	100	100	100	100	100	100	100	100	100	100	1,200
Rent/Mortgage	1,000	1,000	1,000	1,000	1,000	1,000	1,000	1,000	1,000	1,000	1,000	1,000	12,000
Homeowners' Insurance					200							200	400
Savings	0	0	0	0	100	100	100	0	100	100	100	100	700
Utilities	100	100	100	100	100	100	100	100	100	100	100	100	1,200
Vacation									1,500				1,500
House Maintenance	200	100	100	100	100	100	100	100	100	100	100	100	1,300
Cash and Miscellaneous	200	300	300	200	300	300	300	300	200	200	200	400	3,200
TOTAL PERSONAL EXPENSES	3,230	2,880	3,030	2,930	3,680	3,230	3,330	2,880	4,950	3,250	2,700	3,350	39,440

BUSINESS EXPENSES													
Association Dues	1,000												1,000
Bus. Cards, Name Badge	200												200
Auto Expenses	200	200	200	200	200	200	200	200	200	200	200	200	2,400
Long Distance Phone	25	25	25	50	50	50	50	50	50	50	25	25	475
Training	250	250	200	100	100	100	100	100	100	100	100	100	1,600
Internet and Technology	25	25	25	25	25	25	25	25	25	25	25	25	300
Postage and Mailings	100	100	100	100	100	100	100	100	100	100	100	100	1,200
Other Fees	50	50	50	50	50	50	50	50	50	50	50	50	600
TOTAL BUSINESS EXP.	**1850**	**650**	**600**	**525**	**525**	**525**	**525**	**525**	**525**	**525**	**500**	**500**	7,775
TOTAL FAMILY & BUS. EXP.	**5,080**	**3,530**	**3,630**	**3,455**	**4,205**	**3,755**	**3,855**	**3,405**	**5,475**	**3,775**	**3,200**	**3,850**	47,215
MONTHLY CASH FLOW	**−830**	**−30**	**370**	**45**	**−705**	**−255**	**395**	**1,045**	**−1,475**	**675**	**1,250**	**600**	1,085
CUMULATIVE CASH FLOW	**−830**	**−860**	**−490**	**−445**	**−1,150**	**−1,405**	**−1,010**	**35**	**−1,440**	**−765**	**485**	**1,085**	−6,790
Sales Price	150,000	100,000	100,000	100,000	100,000	100,000	150,000	150,000	150,000	150,000	150,000	150,000	1,550,000
Agent A's Commission	2,250	1,500	1,500	1,500	1,500	1,500	2,250	2,250	1,800	2,250	2,250	2,250	22,800
Closings Needed	**1**	**1**	**1**	**1**	**1**	**1**	**1**	**1**	**0.8**	**1**	**1**	**1**	11.8
Sales Needed	**1**	**1**	**1**	**1**	**1**	**1**	**1**	**0.8**	**1**	**1**	**1**	**0**	10.8
Prospects Needed	**5**	**5**	**5**	**5**	**5**	**5**	**4**	**5**	**5**	**5**			49

According to the above numbers, Agent A's financial picture looks like this:

Minimum Sales Goal in Dollars → N49
Agent A's Total Commission →
Closings Needed →
Sales Needed →
Prospects Needed →
Cash Reserve Should Be →
Positive Cash Flow →
Pretax Income →
Year End Cash Surplus →

What 5 things can Agent A do to increase her income?

1
2
3
4
5

also factor the broker's cut, expenses, and dues into the equation. Here's how it all breaks down on the typical $100,000 sale:

a. Home sales price: $100,000

b. Sales commission of 3 percent (b×a): $3,000 (based on a total 6 percent commission)

c. Franchise fee of 6 percent (b×c): $180

d. Proceeds after franchise fee (b−c): $2,820

e. Your split (based on a 50/50 arrangement): $1,410

f. Monthly marketing fee (marketing and desk fees are usually paid monthly, whether you make a sale or not): $100

g. Proceeds after marketing fee (e−f): $1,310

h. Errors and omissions (E & O) insurance (usually paid per sale): $40

i. Your check amount (g−h): $1,270

j. Prepaid training fees and other charges (approximate): $300

k. Your net commission (i−j): $970

Knowing how commissions work will help you be more realistic about your goals, so create a spreadsheet to figure out what your average commission would be. You'll need to know in advance the franchising fee, marketing fees, insurance, and other fees.

Outlining Your Key Goals

At this point you know how much money you need to survive and how much to expect from a typical sale in your area. The next step is to figure out your key goals. You need to project approximately how many prospects you need to talk to in order to make your earning goals. "You probably have no idea how many prospects you need before you make a sale, but you'll get better with time," says Fletcher, who advises new agents to assume ten prospects for every sale. "As you get better at qualifying the buyer your ten-to-one ratio will improve. You should have your first commission check within ninety days of joining an office."

Agents should fill in Worksheet 2-1 during the planning process, then follow up with it regularly to make sure they're meeting or beating their initial projections.

WORKSHEET 2-1: OUTLINE OF KEY GOALS

1. I plan to have my broker interviews completed by _____.

2. I plan to have my license placed by _____.

3. Therefore I should have my first commission check by _____.

4. Which means I should have my first sale by _____.

5. Since my first commission check will average about _____ and will close thirty days from the contract date, I need to make my first sale by _____ (month).

6. This means I must talk to _____ qualified prospects by _____.

This initial projection, along with the financial calculations you've already made, is enough to begin your business plan. The next step is to start outlining your business.

Outlining Your Business Plan

Business plans range in size and scope from a few sheets of paper to a book about the size of the text that you have in your hand right now. It all depends on how much time and effort you want to put into it, and what you want to get out of it. Somewhere in between is probably best, with the words and figures organized in a logical, understandable fashion.

For help, you might want to check out one of the many business planning software programs and plan samples available on the market today, though not all of them are applicable for small, boutique businesses like real estate. Some of them may not be thought provoking enough to create a viable plan for you, since your status as a real estate agent is very different from any other kind of business. On one hand you're accountable to a higher power (that of your broker, followed by your state's real estate associations and licensing entities), yet on the other you're a free spirit, able to make or break yourself.

Even the sample real estate business plan linked to the U.S. Small Business Administration's Web site is geared more toward opening a brokerage than to starting up as a sales associate. With that in mind, we'll take a look at a basic business plan (which you can adapt to your specific business), along with any relevant, industry-specific notes and advice where applicable.

Before you sit down to write out your hopes, dreams, and plans, it may help to envision an audience for your masterpiece—someone else reading your plan (such as an investor, or a bank that you've approached for a line of credit)—while you're writing it. This will help ensure that the document is both clear and concise, and that no important elements are overlooked. If you need help filling in any of the sections, check Appendix A of this book for sample new-agent and existing-agent business plans.

Here are thirteen items that you should include in your business plan.

1. *Cover Sheet:* This page should reflect the image of your new company and include any logos or graphics that you plan to use during the course of business. Use "Business Plan for _____" as the title, and be sure to date the plan.

2. *Table of Contents:* For future reference and for the sake of others who will read your plan, be sure to list each section and subsection throughout the plan.

3. *Executive Summary:* This is a one- to two-page summary of your business plan, so you may want to write it after you've completed the plan. Summarize the key points covered in the plan and include a complete-but-brief overview of your plan. You'll also want to discuss your new business and your goals, such as:

> *I will hang my license at ABC Realty, Inc. and become an independent contractor working under the broker of record at this agency, serving as a trusted adviser and facilitator for buyers and sellers of residential real estate. My goal is to work as either a buyer's agent (working solely with buyers), seller's agent (working solely with those consumers wishing to list their homes), or a combination of the two, and close X number of transaction sides (the buy or sell side of the deal) annually in order to earn X number of dollars in commissions a year.*

4. *Industry/Market Analysis:* When you write this section, pretend that the person who reads your plan knows nothing about your company or its industry. Make it as basic as possible, and answer the following questions:

❑ What is the size of the industry? (Measured by data like the number of existing and new homes sold in your area in a given year, population growth, etc.)

❑ How quickly is the industry growing? (You can usually obtain such statistics from your local Multiple Listing Service or Realtor organization.)

❑ What are the typical profit margins? (Or, how much can I expect to pocket on any given deal after paying my broker's cut and any expenses?)

❑ Who are the major players in the industry?

❑ What are some of the trends and forecasts for the industry? (NAR and most state and local Realtor associations track key data pertaining to the real estate field, as do publications like the *REAL Trends* newsletter, which can be found at www.realtrends.com.)

❑ What changes are occurring in the industry that will create new opportunities for companies such as yours? (The proliferation of discount and Internet brokers has spawned a new interest in experienced, full-service brokers, for example.)

5. *Business Overview:* Here you will describe the products or services that you'll be selling (which in your case will comprise assistance with buying or selling homes), how long your company has been in operation, and a few of its short-term and long-term business goals. Focus on brief, concise descriptions in this section, and keep it limited to one or two pages. Avoid a

lot of industry jargon, and—as suggested earlier—write it for someone who knows nothing about real estate. If you're going to use your business plan to seek out financing (or backing), you'll also want to detail what such funds will be used for (office equipment, vehicle, development of an online presence, first year's worth of rent, etc.).

6. *Ownership and Legal Structure:* This will probably be fairly easy, since most agents start out as sole proprietorships and run their companies solo. However, if your company is in growth mode or has reached the point at which incorporation or partnerships come into the picture, you'll want to adjust your plan to reflect this status. In chapter 8 you'll find more in-depth discussion on these topics.

7. *Management and Staffing:* Someone has to make this plan work, and all of those duties simply aren't going to fall on your shoulders forever. Real estate teams (in which a number of licensed and nonlicensed professionals band together and share the duties) are popular, as is the hiring of full- and part-time assistants and even "virtual" assistants, who work from a remote location. Start this section with a short paragraph detailing your own staffing aspirations (even if you're a one-man show right now), describe what roles those team members or employees will fill in your growing business, and detail your plans for adding human resources to your operation as it grows and prospers.

8. *Marketing Plan:* This section is particularly important for real estate agents, who can't simply sit in their offices and wait for business to come their way. Competition is too stiff and there are entirely too many real estate offices vying for buyers' and sellers' business to operate in this fashion. For that reason, chapter 3 of this book is devoted to your marketing plan. Within your overall business plan you can also insert a few paragraphs detailing your marketing efforts, such as:

- ❏ What you're selling
- ❏ Why customers want and/or need it
- ❏ How you will reach those customers
- ❏ How you will do business with those customers
- ❏ How your services will be priced
- ❏ What your competition looks like
- ❏ Your competitive advantage

9. *Operational Plan:* This section is geared more toward product businesses (such as manufacturers) but is still applicable to real estate agents, who can touch on the following points when filling out this part of the plan:

- ❏ How the business is (or will be) run
- ❏ Where the company is (or will be) based
- ❏ Where the bulk of the work will be handled
- ❏ What tools or resources you will need, and which ones you already have to run the business

10. *Financial Plan:* Kick this section off with the words *level of funding needed* to get the business rolling or growing, and go from there. Fill in an honest assessment of how much money you'll need to get this business off the ground, outline how that money will be used, and provide a valid reason for making those expenditures. Include any historical financial statements, such as the past three years' balance sheet, income, and cash flow statements (if applicable). Also in this section you'll want to develop two to three years' worth of projections based on the goals and action steps that you wrote down and reviewed earlier in this chapter.

11. *Business Strengths and Weaknesses:* What's truly great and innovative about what you're doing, and what areas could

use a little help? Stick to three or four solid strengths that will make you stand out in the marketplace, and be as specific as possible. Rather than writing down a statement like, "I provide great customer service" (which pretty much every company boasts these days), instead write, "I will lease a moving van at a moment's notice and loan it to a customer for use during the moving process." Be equally as specific about your weaknesses, and then think about what you can do to overcome these issues. If you're time strapped and unable to answer e-mail inquiries within a few hours, for example, your solution may be to hire a part-time assistant to man the computer.

12. *Growth Projections:* To complete this section, you'll want to first answer the following questions:

- ❏ Where do I see my company and myself in one year?
- ❏ Where will I be in five years?
- ❏ What will it take to reach these goals?
- ❏ Are these goals attainable in my industry? (Do some research, talk to other agents and brokers, and form a consensus from a number of different sources.)
- ❏ Can my market support these growth projections? (Research your market by looking at new-home building, sales growth of existing homes, and the number of new agents/brokers who come into the business on an annual basis.)
- ❏ Will I need to cultivate new niches (such as working with unmarried or multicultural home buyers) to reach my goals?
- ❏ What type of year-over-year sales increases and growth projections will come as a result of my taking these steps?

13. *Exit Strategy:* What, you say, create an exit strategy when I haven't even gotten my feet wet in the business yet? Ask any business experts and they'll tell you that having a Plan B and even a Plan C can mean the difference between success and failure in the business world. Creating an exit strategy early in the process doesn't mean you're ready to give up. It means you're ready to embrace anything that comes your way, and that you're truly ready to treat your practice like a business and not a hobby.

"An exit strategy is critical, but it's something that very few entrepreneurs think about when they're writing their first business plan," says one professor of entrepreneurship at a large U.S. college. "They're so concerned with getting their companies off the ground, and making payroll, that they overlook the need for an exit strategy."

Here are a few quick tips for creating an exit strategy:

- ❏ If you can't lay out an exit strategy in writing, at least have a few alternative plans in mind, should things not go as planned with your new business.
- ❏ Consult with an attorney, CPA, financial planner, or other professional (preferably a team of professionals) to help develop a viable exit strategy.
- ❏ Take the time to develop an exit strategy, even if you have to take a few hours or days away from your day-to-day business operations to do it. It will pay off.
- ❏ Don't forget to sit down and talk with your spouse and/ or family members (particularly those who work for or have a stake in the business) before creating your exit strategy.
- ❏ Create an exit strategy as early as possible (preferably when you draw up your first business plan), then tweak it as necessary as your company blossoms and grows.

When outlining your business plan, you may want to also incorporate one or more of the following points:

❏ Protection such as licenses, trademarks, or copyrights.

❏ Timing of major operations, such as a business expansion, hiring of employees, forming a team, or launching your Web site.

❏ A set of assumptions, such as anticipated sales volume, cost of goods sold, and gross profit, and data from trade associations (home sales, new home sales, number of competitors in the market).

❏ Projected income statements—monthly for three to five years, then quarterly for three to five years.

❏ Projected cash flow statements—monthly for two years and quarterly for the following three to five years.

❏ A break-even analysis for your business, showing at exactly what point you will reach profitability. For some agents, this can come as quickly as two months into the business. For others, it may take six to twelve months to reach this level.

Once you've completed your first draft of the business plan, you'll want to review it with either a friend, a business associate, a Service Corps of Retired Executives (SCORE) member, or a Small-Business Development Center (SBDC) counselor. The business plan is a flexible document that should change as your business grows. It can be used to get financing, to take your company to the next level, or simply to help you feel confident in your own ability to run a business. Treat it like a first draft, and use the feedback gathered to create a final document.

Stoking Growth

Good business planning isn't limited to brand new agents. Existing agents should also do their share of planning to make sure their enterprises are growing and prospering to their fullest potential. Patti Brotherton, president of PAB Performance Partners in Santa Barbara, California, works regularly with different types of business owners and often wonders to herself: Why is it that real estate agents who have multimillion-dollar enterprises in terms of revenue, don't plan? "You don't have to write a novel, just look at what's been and plan what's to be," Brotherton says.

Look first at the number of closed transactions for the prior year by property address. You want to know if the commission was generated from the buyer side or listing side, what the sales price was, and the amount of commission earned. From this you can determine your average sales price.

Next, examine just the number listings taken for the prior year. Again, you want to note these by property address, date sold or time taken off the market, and the reason that a property didn't sell. This will tell you the percentage of listings sold compared to listings taken, and will help you determine exactly how productive you've been over the last few months.

Last, look at your sources of business. Determine this by listings taken and also by buyer-controlled sales. Note by property address what the source of the business was (a farm, For Sale By Owner, referral, etc.), and after you've gathered the data, use Worksheet 2-2 to analyze it.

WORKSHEET 2-2: BUSINESS ANALYSIS

1. Business Analysis Year _____

2. Total Commissions Earned (Gross) _____

Listing Side:

3. Number of Listings Taken_____

4. Number of Listings Sold_____

5. Percentage of Listings Sold to Listings Taken (line 4 divided by line 3) _____

6. Total Dollar Volume of Listings Sold_____

7. Average Sales Price (line 6 divided by line 4) _____

Selling Side:

8. Number of Buyer-Controlled Sales_____

9. Total Dollar Volume of Buyer-Controlled Sales_____

10. Average Sales Price of Buyer-Controlled Sales (line 9 divided by line 8) _____

Unit Totals:

11. Number of Listings Sold_____

12. Number of Buyer-Controlled Sales_____

13. Total Closed Units_____

Average Income per Unit:

14. Total Commissions Earned (from line 2) _____

15. Total Closed Units (from line 13) _____

16. Average Commission Earned per Unit (line 14 divided by line 15) _____

17. Percentage of Income from Listings Sold (line 6 divided by line 14) _____

18. Percentage of Income from Buyer-Controlled Sales (line 9 divided by line 14) _____

Now that you know where you have been, you can start planning. Did most of your sales come from your listings selling? Did you get your listings from farming? Or, were you equal in listings selling and buyer-controlled sales? Were there many referrals? Where did they come from?

"It's so much easier to plan if you can see an analysis of past performance right in front of you," says Brotherton. You'll also want to look at your expenses. Do they correlate with where your business comes from? In other words, are you spending the most in an area where you are getting the most business? If not, consider spending more where you get your business and less in other areas. In return, you should see your company's revenue go up and its expenses level off.

Don't forget to look at your marketplace and any changes that may have taken place within that market over the last twelve months. Do you think it is the same as last year? Do you think that doing the same activities will net you the same result? "If you do not add to your activities, you can bet that you will not increase your revenue," says Brotherton. "The key is to put your marketing dollars where you get the most business. Increase your activities there, but don't try to spend more in other areas at this time, when you are obviously getting good results from a specific area."

Remember that good planning is more than just getting words on paper or on your computer screen: It requires thought and should provoke you to think about your business and its future. Use a calendar to plan your activities, your spending, and your time, and remember that you have only twenty-four hours in a day to do all of these business activities and live your life.

"Creating your own business plan doesn't take days—but it does involve some analysis of what you are doing," says Brotherton. "The best performers plan, and I coach top agents to spend one to three days on the process, brainstorming and getting focused on what will bring them the most rewards—sales and time off."

Those brainstorming sessions usually surprise agents, as most had an idea of where their business was coming from but never took the time to sit down and really figure out their sources of income, whether their marketing and advertising investments were actually paying off and then contributing to those income streams.

"Some agents know from month to month, but I think that is a rare agent," says Brotherton, who adds that most top performers are "too busy" making sales. "Imagine how much more they would do if they knew absolutely where to spend their time. When you have a business plan written down—along with your goals for the next 12 months—you have all the makings for a tremendously successful year."

CHAPTER THREE

Developing a Marketing Plan

''If you have accomplished

all that you have planned for yourself,

you have not planned enough.''

—Edward Everett Hale

Every good real estate agent has a marketing plan in place. It could be a well-defined, documented plan, or a mental awareness as to which three marketing tools work best for that agent and why. Because your marketing plan communicates how you will reach your customer, you'll want to put some extra emphasis into this section of your business plan. In this chapter, we break the marketing section of your business plan into a separate entity, since it's such an integral part of any agent's success.

Just a few years ago, John Prescott was a brand new agent in a community where he knew no one. A year later, this North Carolina–based agent was the number one agent in the market and had doubled his production from the previous year. "I knew from running businesses that you have to spend money to make money," says Prescott. "You can make the quantum leap or you can take ten years to get there. I decided to get there quicker."

To make that happen, Prescott relied on his background in marketing and advertising in the grocery industry and a seminar given by Hobbs/Herder Training of Newport Beach, California. Once he returned home, the first thing he did was hire an assistant. He then established a separate bank account and deposited enough money to cover three months' salary for his assistant. "Everything I did, I asked myself if I could delegate it," he says. He then trained his new assistant on the systems he had learned at the seminar, allowing him to focus on developing his marketing plan and building his business.

For Prescott, that meant developing a farm area and using direct mail to reach out to 1,500 homes throughout the Brevard, Florida, area. He quickly saw results and closed twenty-five transactions in his first year in the business. In a town where only 400 homes sell each year, Prescott's level of success ranked him as the top agent in town. In 2003, Prescott closed fifty transactions for a total of $10 million in sales. To keep his company growing, he uses a mix of TV commercials and image ads and recently launched his own Web site.

That Prescott attained success fairly quickly in the real estate industry can be chalked up to his willingness to map out a marketing plan, educate himself (apart from the initial agent courses one must take to become a licensed Realtor), and create a business that has made him somewhat of a celebrity in his town. "My dad has lived in this town twelve years longer than I have," says Prescott, "but if we walk down the street together, the people all know me and say hello."

Failing to Plan

Having an overall business plan is one thing, but in real estate a marketing plan can play a critical role in an agent's success. It's easy to get caught up in all of the new options, gadgets, and gizmos available on the market today without properly assessing each of them. As a result, agents end up throwing money and valuable time out the window in their quest to find the best marketing tactic, most effective advertising method, or best promotional tool.

When creating your plan—something most agents will tell you that they have, even if they don't—remember that a plan isn't really a plan unless it's written down. You need a well-thought-out, strategic business plan committed in writing before you can do anything else. Consider any other small business. Say you were opening a store or a restaurant and seeking a bank loan to help get it off the ground. The first thing the bank is going to ask for is to see your business plan, yet almost no real estate agents have a written plan.

Planning is crucial in many ways and helps agents hone the following key points before getting into business:

- ❏ It helps you set goals for yourself.
- ❏ It provides specific direction for your business.
- ❏ It helps you get a handle on exactly where your business is headed.
- ❏ It provides a roadmap for where you're going and how you're going to get there.

"Without a plan," says Greg Herder, CEO of Hobbs/Herder Training in Newport Beach, California, "agents often end up jumping from one strategy to another and never making any real progress as a result." And although a complete business plan is important, the marketing component is particularly crucial for agents. It's equally as important for large companies.

"Marketing is at the root of the success for many of today's leading companies," says Herder. Just look at your television for proof. During the 2002 Winter Olympics, Nike frequently ran a ninety-second commercial that Herder says was one of the best commercials he's ever seen. The commercial had no voiceover and it told the audience nothing about its shoes.

"It just was ninety seconds of pure athletic passion, showing everyone from bridge jumpers to long jumpers, anonymous kickboxers to Vince Carter of the Toronto Raptors, wearing their Nike shoes and gear," says Herder. "Nike paid three times the rate of a normal thirty-second spot, but it worked. I know it made me want to get up off the couch and go buy some new Nikes."

The important thing for agents who are not operating on Nike-size budgets to remember is that mailing a generic post-card once per quarter is not marketing—it's wasting money. Marketing is creating an image and consistently delivering that message to a desired audience. When home owners continue to receive your materials, you're planting that seed in their heads.

"Maybe they're not going to move for five years. Maybe they're going to sell next month. You never know," Herder explains. "That's why the best approach is consistent marketing over the long haul."

Taking the long-haul approach requires a consistently powerful message, delivered in a package that's convenient for the customers. Every time they open their mailbox and see your name, logo, and photo on a mailing, for example, it shows them that you are a professional. It ingrains your image on their psyche. At the time, they may not even be thinking about calling a real estate agent to list their home, but that doesn't matter. What matters is that you're becoming their agent of choice before they actually need your services.

So when the day arrives and they're ready to move, your potential customers will remember your name and image. "And just like the detergent," says Herder, "suddenly they'll find themselves saying, 'Oh yeah, (Your Name Here) specializes in our area. She's huge around here.'"

Assessing the Competition

One of the first things any good business owner does before getting into business is to assess the competition. That's because in order to succeed in the marketplace, you simply must know what else is out there, and how you can both stand head and shoulders above the rest and leverage their individual strengths to your advantage. The latter is particularly relevant for real estate agents, who cooperate with other agents in the marketplace to get deals closed.

Ultimately, your own marketing plan must meet a customer need in a way that's somehow better than your competition. Here are the key issues to consider during this assessment process:

❏ Who your competitors are, where they're located, how long they've been in the business, and (if possible) just how successful they've been in the market over the last twelve to twenty-four months
❏ Your competitors' strengths and weaknesses
❏ An idea of what your competitors are planning to do next (keeping up with trade journals and participating in activities at your local trade association are good ways to stay in the loop)
❏ Your competitors' spending trends

Going a step further, new businesses should also do a thorough competitive analysis prior to opening their doors, in an effort to truly understand the competitive nature of the business and where they stand in the marketplace. Here are the six points that should be covered in the competitive analysis:

1. Who are your five nearest direct competitors?
2. Who are your indirect competitors?
3. Is the competitors' business growing, steady, or declining?
4. What can you learn from their operations or from their advertising?

5. What are their strengths and weaknesses?

6. How does their product or service differ from yours?

Start a file on each of your competitors, including advertising, promotional materials, and pricing strategies, and review these files periodically, determining how often they advertise, sponsor promotions, and offer sales. Study the copy used in the advertising and promotional materials, as well as their sales strategies.

If you're unsure of where to go for some of this information, check out the following resources:

❏ *Internet:* The Internet is a powerful tool for finding information on a variety of topics. It's a great source of competitive intelligence on your market, competitors, and customers.

❏ *Personal Visits:* Visit your competitors' locations if possible. Observe how employees interact with customers. What do their premises look like? How are their products displayed and priced?

❏ *Talking to Customers:* You're probably in regular contact with customers and prospects, but so are your competitors. To learn what your customers and prospects are saying about your competitors, just ask them.

❏ *Competitors' Ads:* Look carefully at competitors' ads to learn about their target audience, market position, product features, and benefits, prices, etc.

❏ *Speeches or Presentations:* Attend speeches or presentations made by representatives of your competitors.

❏ *Trade Show Displays:* View your competitor's display from a potential customer's point of view. What does the display say about the company? Observing which specific trade shows or industry events competitors attend provides information on their marketing strategy and target market.

❏ *Written Sources:* Study publications such as:
  ○ General business publications
  ○ Marketing and advertising publications
  ○ Local newspapers and business journals
  ○ Industry and trade association publications
  ○ Industry research and surveys
  ○ Computer databases (available at many public libraries)

Once you've gathered the pertinent information, plug it into the following competitive analysis:

❏ *Names of Competitors:* List all of your current competitors and research any that might enter the market during the next year.

❏ *Summary of Each Competitor's Products:* This should include location, quality, advertising, staff, distribution methods, promotional strategies, customer service, etc.

❏ *Competitors' Strengths and Weaknesses:* List their strengths and weaknesses from the customer's viewpoint. State how you will capitalize on their weaknesses and meet the challenges represented by their strengths.

❏ *Competitors' Strategies and Objectives:* This information might be easily obtained by getting a copy of their annual report. It might take analysis of many information sources to understand competitors' strategies and objectives.

❏ *Strength of the Market:* Is the market for your product growing sufficiently so there are enough customers for all market players?

Once completed, this exercise should provide you with a clear idea of what you're up against in the industry, gaps in the market that are aching to be filled by a good agent, and exactly how you can create a business that stands heads and shoulders above the competition.

Creating Your Plan

Becoming top of mind in a competitive marketplace starts with a good marketing plan that covers—at minimum—the following components. Many of these issues are typically covered in the market analysis section of a standard business plan.

❏ *An Overview of Your Target Market:* Here's where you'll dig down and find out the nitty-gritty details of your market. Getting this done before you start doing business is optimal, but if you're already working, by all means, do it now. With this information at hand, you'll be able to better determine exactly where your services fit into the market, or what you'll need to do to tweak your plan to better serve that market's needs. When completing this section, be sure to include the following:
- ○ Current population and population growth
- ○ Number of homes, and number of homes constructed annually
- ○ Demographics of your customer base (generally available from your city's economic development department, online at the Bureau of Labor Statistics [www.bls.gov], or from related sources) and answers to these questions:
  - ✧ Are they male or female?
  - ✧ Are they single or do they have families?
  - ✧ What race and ethnic backgrounds are most prominent in my area?
  - ✧ How old are my primary, secondary, and tertiary

client bases? (For example, empty nesters have different housing needs than, say, younger families.)

- ✧ Where do these potential clients work and what are their annual average incomes?

❑ *An Outline of Your Service Strategy:* Since you're a real estate agent, we'll assume that you can pretty much focus in on your service strategy as opposed to worrying about a product strategy. In this section you'll describe in as much detail as possible how your service is different from that of your competitors (who include not only agents working for another brokerage, but also those agents sitting on either side of you in the office). When developing this strategy, ask yourself the following questions:

- ○ Which service offerings are most important to my customers? (Do they need help with the entire real estate transaction, for example, or are they well versed in the process and simply in need of fee-based services like holding open houses and showing their home to prospective buyers?)
- ○ Are customers willing to pay a premium for these services, and will they continue paying a premium in exchange for my services in this realm? (Be sure to factor in the dynamic qualities of a real estate market. Realize that it is indeed cyclical in nature and dependent on a number of economic factors, including interest rates, home-value appreciation, and stock market performance.)
- ○ What will the customer value over the long-term, and how can I center my services on these wants and needs?
- ○ Why would a customer switch to my services? (Consider, for example, someone who may have been

working with an agent who is a close friend or relative.)

○ How will I retain customers so that they won't stray to
another agent in the future? (Many agents believe in
using a combination of e-mail and mail to reach out to
past clients at least once a month, for instance.)

○ What type of ongoing support will I provide to customers to make sure they come back to me when it's time
to buy or sell?

❑ *Details on Your Pricing Approach:* What you jot down for
this section is highly dependent on what type of broker you've
chosen to hang your license with. Commissions are negotiable,
according to real estate license law, but it's generally the broker who establishes a set point that the agents use in the office.
There are exceptions to the rule, of course, but for the most
part agents offer their services at 5 to 7 percent of the sales
price, depending on geographic location. You'll need to look
around in your own market and talk to the broker about your
own pricing approach, since policies can include:

○ *A Full-Service Broker:* Generally charges between 5 and
7 percent of the sales price, with the total amount divided between the agent and the broker (on a predetermined scale, which differs from broker to broker).

○ *A Full-Service, 100-Percent Broker:* These companies
charge the same market rates, but 100 percent of the
commission goes to the agent. This gives the agent a
bit more leeway in determining their price, though
most stick to the going rate in the market unless the
situation warrants a different arrangement.

○ *A Discount, Online, or Flat-Fee Broker:* These are the
new brokerages that have come on the scene since
the introduction of the Internet as a platform for buying and selling homes. All of them have their own set

pricing strategies, which range from 2 percent commissions to a flat fee. If you've hung your license at
one of these shops, your broker will provide the details you need to fill in this pricing section of your marketing plan.

○ *A Broker That Offers Menu Options:* This is a hybrid
between a full-service and discount broker, the latter
of which came to be when someone realized that not
all consumers need or want full service from their
agents. With menu options, an agent offers his services
in exchange for a flat fee, such as $2,000 to handle sev-
eral open houses or $2,500 to draw up contracts for
the sale. Brokers and agents generally work out the
details among one another before offering such services.

❏ *Your Advertising and Promotion Plans:* Getting your name
and face out into the public that will eventually become your
customer base is critical for new agents, particularly those who
come into the business without an established sphere of influence (a group of people who are ready and willing to buy and
sell homes, or who will point customers in your direction).
Here are some key questions to consider when completing this
important section of your marketing plan:

○ *What are the best, most affordable ways that I can start
promoting my business right now?* Consider simple, in-
expensive ways to start getting the word out. Handing
out business cards, putting a sign on the side of your
car, and simply talking about your new career are all
good starting points.

○ *What resources do I have at my avail that will cost little
to reach?* Business clubs, chambers of commerce, and
networking meetings are a good start.

○ *How can I get free publicity?* Local daily and weekly

newspapers and other media outlets frequently run stories on successful businesspeople in the community. Since your audience will probably be mainly local (usually the norm, unless you're in a market where second-home buyers are most prevalent), this is a perfect way to raise public awareness of your business.

○ *Can I sponsor teams, events, or programs?* Little League teams, soccer clubs, and other community programs are always on the lookout for sponsors. In my hometown, for example, a $500 donation to our local soccer club yields the donor a large, banner-size ad on the fence at a club. This is the spot where hundreds of parents and children spend their weekends and weekday evenings in the fall and winter months.

○ *Should I advertise in the phone book?* The short answer is yes, but just how much you want to invest in what size/type of ad depends on a few key factors. Most consumers select agents on reputation, word of mouth referrals from friends and family, or past experiences with that agent. Ask around your office and community about the value of a phone book listing, and then decide what will work best for you.

○ *How can I use the Internet as a marketing tool?* If you're a new agent, then the Internet is your oyster, particularly when it comes to netting buyers. Entrenched agents also reap the rewards of an Internet presence. Both types of agents are using the following strategies online right now:

✧ Individual agent and broker Web sites

✧ Broker reciprocity or IDX (Internet Data Exchange) (systems that allow a broker to display all of the listings from specific MLS areas on her Web site)

✧ Popular online data aggregators, such as Realtor

.com, where home buyers and sellers go to either list their homes or view homes

✧ Lead generation sites (such as HomeGain.com or HouseHunt.com), some of which offer "exclusive" territories to agents in exchange for a fee, then feed those agents customer leads in their respective regions

❏ *Your Overall Sales Strategy:* In this section you'll tie together all of the other components mentioned above into one succinct description of your company's sales strategy. New agents can stick to the basics in this section, but existing agents who are looking to grow their companies may have more information to add. Basically, you'll want to look at what you (and any of your employees or assistants) are going to do to boost your company's sales, and how you're going to handle growth once it becomes too much for one person to handle. The answers to the following questions will help you fill in this section:

○ How many salespeople do I need (other than myself) right now?

○ How many will I need one year from now, should I reach my sales goals over the next twelve months?

○ What kind of customer support do I need to offer, and how does this level of customer service affect my overall sales?

○ When the time comes, will I hire employees, or can I outsource some of these services to a virtual assistant? (Keep an eye on state licensing laws, as most have set forth guidelines governing the work of licensed versus unlicensed assistants.)

○ What other sales support do I need to have in place in order to reach my financial and life goals?

❏ *Approximate Marketing Budget:* One of the most challenging tasks facing small-business owners is just how much money to invest in marketing and advertising themselves and their company to the world. Spend too much and you risk going into the red financially. Spend too little and what little you did spend will be for naught, since customers won't know that you exist. In this section, you'll review your marketing needs versus your financial resources and decide just how much money to allocate on a weekly or monthly basis for marketing. Remember that this will be a moving target, since a few good commission checks can free up extra cash for advertising, but coming up short can find you holding back on the purse strings for a few months. The key is to deliver a consistent, steady message to the public about your services and do it in a manner that's both affordable and effective.

There's no specific formula for developing a marketing budget, though most companies use a basic percentage-of-sales approach. They compare advertising expenditures to actual sales results as follows:

- First year: 10 percent of projected sales
- Second year: 7 percent of projected sales
- Third year and beyond: 5 percent of projected sales

Keep in mind that this is a formula that applies to all businesses, and that real estate by nature is an advertising-intensive industry that has higher-than-usual advertising needs.

Being Real Estate Specific

When drafting your marketing plan, you'll also want to factor in a few real estate–specific points that will help you get a handle not only on your budget, but also on the effectiveness of your methods and choices. That way, the next time a salesperson from a homes magazine tries to sell you advertising, you'll have a good Idea of whether the investment is worth your time, energy, and money. The first step is to objectively review your marketing strategies from the consumer's point of view. "Agents don't inherently take this step," says Herder. Instead, they come up with generalizations like:

> *If I'm a better agent than the one who sold me my house, then I'll be able to do a better job.*

Or:

> *I'm going to build my marketing around service.*

Understand that such statements are too general, and that most consumers don't actually discern between agents in terms of experience (unless they're already acquainted with them or have worked with them in the past), but that they tend to lump all licensed agents (and even those who are members of the national, state, and regional Realtor associations) into one category, assuming that because they're licensed that they must be adequately qualified and knowledgeable.

To better sharpen up your own marketing message, use your marketing plans to build your positioning or point of difference in the market. Ask yourself the following questions:

- ❏ What is my target market (outlined above in the first section of your marketing plan) buying right now?
- ❏ What needs and wants are driving their purchasing decisions?

❏ Knowing these needs, wants, and habits, what can I provide to these customers that no other agent can?

❏ How can I maximize these differentiations in the marketplace in an effective, affordable manner?

❏ What are my own strengths and weaknesses, and how can I capitalize on the strengths and minimize the weaknesses when I'm working in the market?

"What it really comes down to is that you're going to build your positioning on your point of difference," says Herder. "If you take the time to do this, you'll have a leg up on the competition because most agents don't ever analyze their own strengths and weaknesses. Instead, they select methods that are inherently marketing challenged to start with."

The next step is to analyze customer response—or, exactly how your potential or current customers are responding to your marketing methods. If you find that your outgoing personality helps you win friends and influence people, for example, then you'll want to put that personality trait to good use while you're out in the field selling homes. If, on the other hand, customers seem to respond better to your low-pressure, conservative type of personality, then use your character to communicate with customers in a manner that makes them both comfortable and responsive.

"Find something in your personality that you can build your marketing plan on, and make sure your marketing materials reflect those traits and values," Herder advises.

Because each individual agent is different, and because real estate is a fragmented industry where many different types of business models are currently in use, it's difficult to pinpoint even the most basic of marketing strategies without presenting a hypothetical example that you can use as a guide. Here are two very different examples that illustrate a few key real estate–specific marketing strategies.

Example #1:

❏ *Farm Area:* Seacliff Estates

❏ *Number of Homes:* 1,500

❏ *Media Options for This Farm Area:* A newspaper that covers the area, plus 14,000 other homes that you're *not* trying to reach. There is no cable television that covers the area, which means direct mail will probably be a top bet for agents looking to reach out to those home owners. In this case, direct mail will basically dictate the campaign.

Example #2:

❏ *Farm Area:* Pinewood Forest

❏ *Number of Homes:* 10,000

❏ *Media Options for This Farm Area:* A local newspaper that covers the area, a few cable television options, and strategically placed billboards. In this market, the agent has more ways to reach out to a wider audience.

Understand that neither option is better or worse than the other, and this simply shows how vastly different two agents' marketing plans will be. The agent working in a small town where a local newspaper is the only media outlet, and where direct mail is the best choice, for example, isn't necessarily going to do better than the agent who has access to television and billboards to reach out to the audience. That's because the latter may face working in a market where competition for listings and buyers is stiff. It's simply a matter of geography and personal choice. The key is to understand the audience and your place in the market. You then need to leverage your strengths and competitive advantages to get out there and start working with this group.

Sometimes, taking a myopic view of a market can prove disastrous for an agent, as Herder has learned over the years. One of his earliest clients, for example, was a real estate agent who was in need of a good marketing program. She pulled up to Herder's office in a Rolls-Royce® and wore expensive jewelry and clothing. Her broker had assigned her a 500-home farm area, composed mainly of lower-income families. New to the business and eager to put his expertise to work, Herder set out to create a marketing plan for the agent.

Unfortunately, Herder and this agent's myopic view of the market—combined with the socioeconomic differences between the agent and her farm area—equaled failure. "In the ninety days that followed she did twelve listing presentations and didn't sign up a single client," Herder says. "When you go zero for twelve, there's something wrong."

When the pair sat down to assess the marketing plan, Herder says the agent told him she was "scared to death to go out on the listing presentations." He made a call to the broker, telling him there was no way this particular agent would ever succeed in that farm area. Told that there were no higher-end areas available, the agent wound up leaving the real estate industry a year later. "She could have done very well if she would have had a chance to work in an area where she felt comfortable," says Herder.

Sometimes, it works the other way around. An agent with no experience in the luxury home market, for example, will attempt to jump into it with dollar signs in his eyes. Knowing the fat commission checks that come from selling multimillion-dollar homes, he'll spend months trying to get his foot in the door of the mansion on the water. Instead, he would probably be better off selling several midpriced homes a few blocks down the street.

These are precisely the types of challenges you'll avoid by creating a marketing plan, then reviewing it and tweaking it on a regular basis. Factor your target market, your budget, and your progress so far (if applicable) into the mix and you'll avoid the challenges the Rolls-Royce®–driving agent had to deal with. You'll probably wind up with a much longer stint in an industry where 83 percent of home sellers used Realtors to sell 6.1 million homes nationwide in 2003, according to the National Association of Realtors.

Getting Affordable

Flip through your Sunday paper this week and you'll see a plethora of multicolor ads showcasing homes and the agents who have them listed for sale. Grab a home magazine off the free publication pile and you'll get an eyeful of full-page and multipage ads of the same nature. On the Internet, a quick search for agents in your area will reveal a number of elaborate Web sites equipped with virtual tours and broker reciprocity–linked listing data.

Let's face it, marketing and advertising isn't cheap, nor is it always effective. New agents in particular take a gamble when plunking down cash in exchange for a new marketing method, since most lack the benchmarks or historical data needed to make comparisons. And although the agents in your office can be a good source of feedback, one agent's negative feedback concerning the use of "Just Listed" or "Just Sold" postcards doesn't necessarily mean that such direct mail pieces will not work for you.

"Unfortunately, agents are always looking for generalizations," Herder says. "But generalizations are not always available, nor are they always accurate." When figuring a marketing budget, for example, he says most experts agree that an agent should allocate 30 percent of his projected first-year's gross sales to marketing. The number then tails off as the agent progresses in the business. For example:

❏ First year's projected sales: $100,000
❏ First year's marketing budget: $30,000 a year or $2,500 per month (at 30 percent of sales)
❏ Second year's projected sales: $150,000
❏ Second year's marketing budget: $22,500 a year or $1,875 per month (at 15 percent of sales)

Too often, agents skimp on the marketing, particularly during those first couple of lean years. Using the formula above, they underestimate their annual sales and end up spending far too little money to get their companies rolling. "The problem is if you have no sales and you spend 15 percent, you end up with nothing," says Herder. "I usually tell them to handle it how they want to, but I let them know that it's better to come up with a workable budget that fits with their sales expectations."

The good news for agents on a budget is that there are some great marketing tactics out there that don't cost a fortune. Here are some starter ideas to use right now in expanding your client base and spreading the word about your real estate service offerings:

❏ *Get out of your office and start talking to people:* Real estate is very much a word-of-mouth industry, where good news travels fast and bad news travels even faster. Agents tend to be a tightly networked group of individuals who seem to know everyone. To get on that A-list, get out into the community and start schmoozing with people. Spread the word about your business to everyone you meet and hand out business cards. Tell everyone that you're a real estate agent. I once knew an agent who got most of her clients—either directly, or by referral—from the parents she mingled with on a daily basis at her daughter's elementary school.

❏ *Seek out free publicity opportunities:* As mentioned earlier in this chapter, local media outlets are always looking for successful businesspeople to feature in their publications or shows. Since real estate agents tend to be active in their communities, consider associating yourself with a local event, then alert media to the event and your availability for interviews. One successful agent in New York, for example, prides himself on being a prominent figure in the community. He's a patron of the arts. He's sponsored concerts, served on various boards of directors, and volunteered his time to various associations.

❏ *Ask for referrals:* The average agent doesn't properly educate her clients about giving her referrals. When meeting a potential client for the first time, for example, one agent tells the client that she wants to work with people on a win-win basis. She says to them, "If at the end of buying or selling your home you feel I have taken good care of you and given you great value, will you be willing to commit to referring me at least two people during the following twelve months?" She then reinforces that commitment throughout the transaction so that her clients expect to send her referrals. Other ways to ensure referrals include sending out thank you notes for a referral that's received and using a database to track both customers and the referrals.

❏ *Utilize the Internet:* Marketing via e-mail is a flexible, cost-effective, and easy way to reach out to customers on their own terms. It has become a great method of staying in touch with past clients, via short newsletters, updates, new listing announcements, and other tools. E-mail allows you to easily drive traffic to your Web site, reach a broad geographic audience, and stay in frequent contact with your customers and prospects. E-mail marketing allows you to market your services and establish your expertise with your audience. When using e-mail, you'll want to avoid "spamming" customers at all costs by sending messages only to those recipients who have given permission. When someone asks to be removed, respond immediately.

❏ *Think outside of the box:* Don't be afraid to see what people in other industries are doing and adapt that to your business. Think about the little details that will get attention. For example, if you have a buyer who is chomping at the bit for a home in a certain neighborhood where no homes are currently on the market, why not make up a targeted postcard offering to introduce your buyer to a potential seller in that neighborhood? On the Fourth of July, why not go out to your farm area and put U.S. flags in the ground at each home, and include a business card or message identifying you as the agent of choice for that particular area?

For Existing Agents

Much of the information in this chapter is geared to the new agent who needs a concept-to-completion plan of action for marketing herself. But that doesn't mean marketing plans are only for the new and uninitiated. All agents, no matter what level of success they've achieved, need a solid marketing plan in order to learn what works, what doesn't, what needs to be tweaked, and what should be thrown out the window.

Be sure to not only write the plan down, but also review it quarterly and annually, with the latter constituting a more thorough, intensive look at what's working and what's not. Should a plan be changed daily? Absolutely not, since most marketing efforts take time to mature and produce results. However, if your instincts are telling you that a certain strategy (say, a full-page yellow pages ad) isn't producing results, then you'll definitely want to pare down your investment in that area.

One sure sign that your marketing plan needs tweaking is a stagnating business, particularly in a market where your competitors seem to be doing just fine. "If you're not growing at 5 or 10 percent a year, then something is eroding your client base," says Herder. "There should be a steady, upward trend in sales. If there isn't, then it's time to look at your overall business plan and marketing plan to pinpoint the problem."

Things to look at during this exercise include:

- ❏ How much of my business is coming from new clients?
- ❏ How much comes from past clients?
- ❏ How much is coming from referral clients?

If the percentage is heavily weighted on past clients, for example, it could signal the need for better marketing strategies to drum up new business. If your new business pipeline is full but referrals are nonexistent, then it's time to put more effort into asking for the referral rather than just assuming that someone will point a customer in your direction.

By going through this review process on a quarterly basis (reviewing last quarter and comparing it to the same period in the prior year, if possible) and annual basis (looking at the past twelve months and contrasting that against the previous twelve months if those numbers are available), you'll have a much better handle on exactly what you need to do to reach your company's financial goals.

It's all part of good planning. "Planning is the best time investment an agent will ever make," says Herder. "Learning to work *on* your business instead of *in* your business is critical. It takes you from being trapped by your business to actually managing a company that you can be happy with, and that will help you achieve your goals."

CHAPTER FOUR

Setting Goals and Objectives

"IT IS ALWAYS WISE TO LOOK AHEAD,

BUT DIFFICULT TO LOOK FURTHER

THAN YOU CAN SEE."

—SIR WINSTON CHURCHILL

Everyone has goals and objectives, no matter how trivial or undocumented they may be. It could be as simple as getting a grocery order, or as complex as buying a home, but it's still an objective. Without them, everything would get done with no organization, and no way of knowing the benefits and rewards that came from attaining those objectives.

It works the same way in the business world: Without objectives and goals, a business owner never really knows where she stands, what she's accomplished, and what she hopes to attain over the short and long term. Know that there is a difference between goals and objectives:

❏ *Goals* are broad, long-range ideals that a business owner wants to achieve. There are both primary goals (those that you want to achieve) and secondary goals (what you have to do or create to achieve these goals). They're not intended to be specific enough to act on, but simply state an overall ambition.

❏ *Objectives* are more specific targets of performance and what we'll be discussing most in this chapter. Common business objectives include profitability, productivity, and growth. Because you basically are your own business as a real estate agent, your own objectives will also include personal and lifestyle-related issues.

A good way to get your goal- and objective-setting exercise in gear is to take a big-picture look at your overall goals, as defined above. You also want to think about how you'll achieve them and how you'll handle any goals that you do not achieve in the predetermined amount of time. Use Worksheet 4-1 to get these thoughts on paper.

WORKSHEET 4-1: OVERALL GOALS

1. What are my short-term goals? (For the next six to twelve months.)

_____

_____

_____

2. What are my long-term goals? (For the next twelve months to ten years.)

_____

_____

_____

3. Are my goals financially based, satisfaction-based, or a combination of the two?

_____

_____

_____

4. How will my business objectives affect my personal and life goals?

_____

_____

_____

5. How realistic are these objectives?

_____

_____

_____

6. How will I evaluate my success along the way?

_____

_____

_____

7. What will I do if I don't achieve my goals?

_____

_____

_____

If you worked through this and are ready to dig a bit deeper to come up with additional detailed objectives, then you're already miles ahead of the pack in your industry. According to Patti Brotherton, less than 5 percent of all real estate agents set goals. "Sure, they know how much they need to make in order to pay the bills, but they don't actually set goals so that they can strive for ever greater rewards," says Brotherton, who works often with agents, helping them to hone their business skills. "The fact is, we all know that the person who knows where she's going is sure to arrive."

Brotherton herself is so adamant about setting goals that she dedicates two days at the end of each year (or, sometimes, the beginning of the next year) to go off on her own and work on her goals. That includes both long-range goals and those that she'll work to accomplish over the upcoming year. Once back from her retreat, she discusses the goals with her family and starts working on them.

"This process has made such a difference in what I accomplish," she says, acknowledging that not everyone must physically get away to think about what is wanted out of life. However, she does feel that agents need to take stock of where they have been before they can figure out where they are going. During the process, she urges agents to take a holistic approach to setting objectives by looking not only at their business life, but also at their personal and family life.

Right now, you're probably most interested in learning how to set realistic-yet-challenging objectives for your business, whether you've been working in it for one day or five years. The first step is to consider how satisfied you are with your current earnings. Then, consider the time spent generating those earnings, and figure out if you can make the same amount of money in less time. Realize that money is not the only measure of success, and that the agent who works 75 hours a week for $250,000 in commissions annually and the one who works 50 hours a week for $150,000 may both be meeting their objectives.

"There are many different ways to look at your business. Not only in how much you are making, but in the amount of time it is taking and how much it is costing you to bring in that much revenue," says Brotherton. "All of these come into play when you take the time to set goals."

Ask yourself these questions before setting objectives:

❏ Have I planned some time off into my schedule?
❏ Will I be able to take a vacation and recharge?
❏ Am I spending enough time with my family and friends?
❏ Am I spending enough time on myself, taking care of health-related issues and other important aspects of my life?

If you answered no to any of these questions, you'll want to tweak your objectives to include these very important aspects of your life. The level of priority that you give them is a personal choice, but to avoid burnout, health, and family problems, it's advisable that you at least consider your important aspects when setting objectives both for yourself and for your business.

Laying It Out

Now it's time to get your objectives down on paper. We're going to take a look at the business-related points first, although later in this chapter you'll learn more about striking a workable balance in an industry where working weekends is the norm and customers have a direct, 24/7 cell phone link to your ear.

For starters, make a list of everything you want to accomplish—both business and personal. Write down everything imaginable, then start paring it down. It's easy to get overwhelmed during this phase because your list may be very long, but the key is to get yourself down to five solid objectives. "If you have too many, you'll lose focus and become discouraged," Brotherton says. "It's like going to a really great seminar where you hear many ideas that would be beneficial to your business. You come home and because there are so many you don't know which one to do first so consequently, you do nothing!"

When setting objectives, make sure you pick the kind that are:

- ❏ *Specific*, and as detailed as possible
- ❏ *Measurable*, and able to be quantified
- ❏ *Action-oriented*, and not dependent on certain feelings or notions
- ❏ *Realistic*, and attainable within the set amount of time
- ❏ *Timely,* and completed within a certain time frame

When creating your own top objectives, you'll want to avoid lofty, generic objectives like:

- ❏ I want to sell more houses.
- ❏ I want to find new customers.
- ❏ I want to increase my income.
- ❏ I want to do more business than the other agents in my office.

❏ I want more time to myself, away from work.

These types of statements will only drive you crazy. It's like saying that you "want to lose weight." Once your five objectives .are in place, you'll want to write up a plan of action for achieving those objectives, like this:

Example #1: New Agents

❏ *Objective:* I want to increase the number of prospects that I reach on a weekly basis from five to fifteen over the next three months.

❏ *Plan of Action:* Expand my farm area by 250 homes and join two local organizations where I can network and schmooze with potential clients.

Example #2: Existing Agents Wanting to Grow

❏ *Objective:* I want to increase my annual earnings from $25,000 to $40,000 for the upcoming year.

❏ *Plan of Action:* Working backward, and basing the calculations on a 50/50 commission split with my broker on a gross commission rate of 6 percent, I'll need to close an additional $1 million in sales (five $200,000 homes) a year. Based on the assumption that one in twelve contacts turns into a sale, that means making sixty additional contacts (or five per month) throughout the year.

Example #3: Existing Agents Looking to Pare Down Time Spent on Business

❏ *Objective:* By summer, I want to be able to increase the amount of quality time spent with my family and friends by ten hours a week.

❏ *Plan of Action:* I can either hire and train an assistant to handle my non–real estate activities (answering calls, creating Web content, mass mailing postcards, etc.), hire a part-time licensed assistant to handle more of the real estate–related tasks, or contract certain day-to-day tasks to a virtual assistant on a per-project basis.

Pinpoint your objectives, write them down, make them quantifiable, and attach time frames to them. Then refer back to them often to measure your progress and adjust your work and selling style. "Many agents have told me that they have goals, but that they don't write them down," says Brotherton. "When you write down your goals, your subconscious takes over and works on them as well."

Writing down your objectives provides another benefit: At the end of the year, when you take out that list that you worked on for twelve months, you'll know exactly what you did—and did not—accomplish. Expect it to be a rewarding experience, a wake-up call, or something in between.

When creating your business objectives, be sure to cover four key areas within your business:

1. *Finance:* Improving profit and sales, or reducing costs or losses
2. *Customers:* Increasing customer satisfaction, choice, value
3. *Internal Results:* Speeding up the delivery time to customers
4. *Growth and Learning:* Increasing access to knowledge sources and developing organizational skills

Food for Thought

Setting objectives is particularly important for real estate agents, who are usually left to make or break themselves in an intense industry. Although some companies will provide training that goes beyond just selling, you should go into it knowing that self-motivation and discipline will play a key role in your success. Through good planning, you'll be much better prepared to tackle challenges and overcome obstacles that are put in your way.

Use Worksheet 2-2 from chapter 2 to evaluate your sources of business so you can start laying out some important objectives. Here are some questions that will help you look at your business and pinpoint areas where you may need to set some solid objectives for the upcoming months:

- ❏ Did most of your sales come from the sale of your own listings?
- ❏ Did you get your listings from farming?
- ❏ Were you equal in listing and buyer-controlled sales?
- ❏ Were there many referrals?
- ❏ Where did those referrals come from?
- ❏ Do your expenses correlate with where your business comes from?
- ❏ Are you spending the most in the area where you are getting the most business?
- ❏ Is the marketplace climate the same as last year?
- ❏ Will doing the same activities net your business the same result as last year?
- ❏ What marketing activities can you beef up to help increase your revenue and deal with market changes?

When setting objectives, remember that business success is a very subjective term. What's good for one may not be good for another, so don't rely solely on other agents in your office to help shape your objectives. That's not to say you can't use the suggestions of wizened professionals to help you, it simply means that you should take that advice and use it to shape objectives that truly fit your own wants and needs.

Here are some other things to keep in mind as you set and conquer your objectives:

❑ *Be flexible:* You don't want to change your goals and objectives every day, but realize that circumstances beyond your control may cause you to rethink your plan. Adjust it as you see fit, always making sure that your new objectives are in line with your longer-range planning strategies.

❑ *Break it down:* If your plan is too long and hard to digest, break it down into several smaller, more manageable plans that you can sink your teeth into.

❑ *Ask around:* Share your objectives with someone you trust and respect, and ask that person or persons to provide constructive feedback on their feasibility.

❑ *Reward yourself:* What good are goals if they don't come with rewards? Be sure to reward yourself (a weekend upon closing three sales in a thirty-day period, for example) as significant milestones are accomplished.

❑ *Adjust upward:* You want your objectives to be attainable, but not too easy that they no longer motivate you to do better. If you're working through your objectives and reaching your goals in much shorter time frames than predicted, you'll want to set the bar a little higher and give yourself something to work toward.

Staying Fresh

In real estate, setting objectives can do more than just give you something to work for. They can also help you focus and succeed in an industry where burnout and frustration are common, and where a high number of new agents lose their gumption during their first twelve months in business.

Lori Arnold knows how stressful those first few months in business can be on new real estate agents. Arnold often advises those agents to get in the habit of setting goals and objectives for themselves. "This business can be emotionally tough on agents," says Arnold. "It's very easy to get burned out."

By establishing goals, then setting objectives to help yourself reach those longer-term aspirations, you'll be one of the few agents who stay fresh, even when business is tough. "Goals and objectives keep agents excited, and interested in the business," says Arnold. "We all need something to work toward, and to feel like we've truly accomplished something."

Having goals to work toward, and clear objectives to use as ladder rungs in achieving those aspirations, is key in the real estate industry, where the average agent closes seven deals a year. That leaves a lot of downtime between commission checks—lapses that you can work through seamlessly with clearly defined objectives that are set in advance, adjusted accordingly, and used to measure longer-term success on a regular basis.

To set effective objectives, agents should first evaluate why they're in the real estate business in the first place. An agent who got her real estate license to earn a higher income, for example, would have different objectives than the one who signed up because a few family members found success in the business. "You really need to find the reasoning behind your desire to be in real estate, then use that information to drive your objectives and long-term goals," Arnold says.

Agents who have been in the business for two or more years can take a slightly different approach by asking themselves where their customers are coming from, finding ways to better harvest those sources, and finding new ones. Here's an example:

John hung his license at XYZ Realty two years ago and has since seen his commission checks drop to undesirable levels. How can he set better objectives and work toward more effective long-term goals? Simple—he needs to look at where his business is coming from.

Let's say 20 percent of his business came from his own personal contacts or "sphere of influence," 20 percent from inbound and outbound phone calls, and 5 percent from newspaper ads. If John is spending 70 percent of his marketing budget on newspaper ads, then he needs to rework his advertising approach to make better use of the sources that actually bring him business.

For John, that could mean setting an objective to join two new business groups within three months to help expand his sphere of influence, and hiring a part-time assistant to monitor his phone calls while he's on the road and unable to attend to that source of business.

One of the key areas where agents fall behind on their business objectives involves prospecting—or "getting out there" into their communities to find new customers. David Fletcher of Agents Boot Camp regularly works with new and existing agents and says the real culprit behind income fluctuations is not the industry's commission model, but rather the individual agent's ability to prospect and keep the pipeline full of new business. Consistency counts, and can be cultivated by setting solid objectives on even a daily basis.

"To really understand where they're headed, agents should have a daily prospecting objective," says Fletcher, who urges agents to track over time the number of homes they're selling in relation to the volume of new prospects they're contacting. In other words, if you're turning one out of ten contacts into customers, you need to contact a proportionate number of prospects every day to meet your monthly sales goals.

And it's those sales goals that will help you measure your financial success in the industry, whether your goal is to become a multimillion-dollar producer, or simply earn enough income to cover the bills and sock a little bit away for retirement. A recent business survey found that 89 percent of small businesses that grew for three years or more used methods of tracking their business-related goals for growth, income, and expenses.

As a real estate agent, you'll want to join this crowd of entrepreneurs and begin tracking your success right away. Doing so will not only help you outline a clear business path for your new career but will also help you:

❏ React objectively (rather than reactively in a "putting out fires" type of environment) to changing business climates, market conditions, and business challenges

❏ Create a measure by which you can progress toward your objectives and goals

❏ Keep on top of potential problems before they become detrimental to your company

❏ Be less apt to make impulsive decisions that can hurt your business (such as firing an assistant when money is low, rather than figuring out where the dearth is and boosting a part of your business to stimulate financial growth)

Most real estate coaches and experts feel that agents don't do enough to set and achieve objectives during the course of business, and the bulk of agents simply throw out general, unfocused goals (usually at the start of a new year) without figuring out exactly what they need to do to get there. Here are two tools that you can start using right now to develop your own successful plan of attack:

1. *Be clear about exactly what you want:* Most agents don't know what they want, want too much, or are unsure of why they want it. Others are worried about not achieving their goals and objectives, so they shy away from setting them. Remember that you have a 50 percent chance if you try, but a zero percent chance if you don't. Go for the 50/50 chance and see what turns up.

2. *Understand the objective- and goal-setting process:* We've heard the phrase "reach for your goals" our entire lives, but has anyone ever taught you exactly how to go about making that happen? Here are some guidelines you can start using right now in your own business:

> ❏ If failure weren't even possible, what would I want to accomplish over the next twelve months? As mentioned earlier in this chapter, stick to your five most important short-term goals. Be as specific as possible; make them measurable and set deadlines for each. Make each of them just out of reach, but not so far out of sight that they become too difficult to achieve.

> ❏ What will you gain by achieving these objectives? Look at both financial and personal gains and write down as many as you can think of.

> ❏ What will you miss out on by not achieving these objectives? This will be part of your motivation to succeed, so be honest with yourself.

> ❏ What could possibly prevent you from achieving these objectives? By recognizing the obstacles up front, you'll be much better prepared to work through them if and when they're put in front of you.

> ❏ What resources or people can I tap to help achieve these objectives? Everyone from your broker to your family or the agents sitting around you in your office can be facilitators during this process.

❏ What actions or steps can I take right now to start working toward these objectives? Just because your overall business plan isn't complete yet, that doesn't mean you can't start turning your dreams into reality right now.

Getting Personal

Burnout runs rampant in the real estate industry, but that doesn't mean you have to fall prey to this common ailment. It can be averted by integrating your own personal goals and objectives into your business plan. As an agent, you'll not only want to set financial goals for yourself and your company, you'll also want to dig a little deeper and establish some clear objectives for your own personal goals.

Whether you want to run a marathon, plan a family, or go on a seven-day vacation, it's vital that you maintain sight of these personal wants and needs as you build your real estate business into a successful enterprise. It's sometimes easier said than done—particularly when a home closing is scheduled smack in the middle of your Caribbean vacation and can't be changed—but there are ways to get some balance into your hectic real estate career.

Why, you ask, is balance important when you're trying to write up a new business plan or develop better strategies for an existing practice? It's because real estate agents are particularly prone to burnout and overwork, often through no fault of their own. "The public perception is that agents are accessible twenty-four hours a day, seven days a week," says one New Jersey–based agent who has been in real estate fifteen years and closed $11 million worth of business in 2003. She bucks the 24/7 treadmill by working forty-hour workweeks and taking every Sunday off, without fail. She also removed her home number from the Multiple Listing Service system, mostly as a way to keep other agents from disturbing her single day off.

"The worst offenders are other agents," she says. "I used to get agents calling me on Sunday evening for feedback on a property that I showed a week prior. It was ridiculous." She also revels in activities that simply aren't cell-phone friendly— like skiing, leaving the country, and/or vacationing for at least four to six weeks out of the year. "Travel is one of my favorite hobbies," she adds, "and I've learned that it's very hard to get cell service in countries like Mexico."

This agent may know how to draw the line in the sand between work and play, but the typical agent does not. Concerned about missing "the big deal," upsetting a customer, or being left out of a big opportunity, many agents feel they simply must be available 24/7 or risk failure. "Most agents either live in survival mode, scared to miss any business," says Joeann Fossland, CEO of real estate coaching company Advantage Solutions Group in Cortaro, Arizona, "or they neglect to honor their own needs and say no to others, so they end up working fifty to sixty hours a week with no days off."

The technology movement has both helped and hindered the agent's ability to get away. Although agents no longer have to be tied to a desk to take phone calls—nor do they have to do as much driving around with clients (thanks to innovations like the virtual tour), today's agents spend more time monitoring e-mail and connected to cell phones and pagers.

For those agents who find themselves tethered to such devices seven days a week, the first degree of separation is taking off at least one twenty-four-hour period every week. Schedule that time well in advance, Fossland says, and try not to let any business get in the way of your downtime. "Start communicating boundaries to everyone around you, set work hours, and share them with your clients," says Fossland, who also suggests printing official business hours on your business cards and brochures.

Getting your family involved with your work goals can also be beneficial. "Let them know when you'll be available to them, and get them involved in goals—like a trip to Disneyland if you get ten listings this month," she says. "It's a great way to turn the family into cheerleaders, instead of them feeling you are ignoring them."

Agents concerned that a trip to Disneyland without the cell phone could translate into lost business will be surprised to find out that just the opposite is true. In fact, agents who consciously take downtime for themselves tend to be more productive, more enthusiastic, and healthier than their stressed-out counterparts. They're also more choosy about whom they work with.

"Agents who are good at taking time off really don't miss anything," Fossland says. "That's because the agents who think they need 'everything that comes along' tend to work with high-maintenance clients rather than customers who respect their time, and who will wait until tomorrow to see a property."

Here is some sage advice on how to set yourself up for success, not burnout, as a residential real estate agent:

❑ Buy an electronic or hard-copy calendar and start scheduling your personal and family time, then work your real estate commitments in and around those important events.

❑ Take up a hobby, sport, or interest that takes you away from the cell phone or pager for a few hours out of the week. Skiing, boating, and traveling to foreign countries are all good options.

❏ Recognize that you do need a vacation, and schedule one right now.

❏ If you're an overworked solo agent, consider hiring part-time or full-time help to handle mundane tasks that are keeping you from enjoying downtime.

❏ If you can't take a long vacation this year, schedule several minibreaks throughout the year. Weekend getaways are a good way to unwind without being too far out of touch.

❏ Take Sunday (or any another twenty-four-hour period) off every week to rejuvenate and recharge.

❏ On those days when you're "untouchable" (like on those Sundays), don't check e-mail, turn off the pager, and hide the cell phone. Enjoy time with your family or friends, or solitude!

By establishing solid business objectives and goals and setting your sights on a leading a balanced, fulfilling life, you'll be more apt to enjoy your position as a real estate agent, reach your short- and long-term goals, and attain the level of success that you've set forth for yourself.

CHAPTER FIVE

Managing a Fluctuating Income

''A good plan today is better

than a perfect plan tomorrow.''

—George S. Patton

When you sign up for a sales career based solely on commissions, it doesn't take long to uncover the positives and negatives of the setup. On one hand, your paychecks are sizable, and unlimited in that there is no real ceiling prohibiting you from earning as much as you can. The checks can also come more frequently than the average paycheck, with some agents closing multiple deals per week based on the number of deals they do during a particular time period.

On the other hand, these checks are not always guaranteed, nor do they come at a predictable rate. One month you may take home $7,000 in commissions, for example, and the next you may find yourself coming up empty. These are the natural ebbs and flows of working on commissions, and they come with the territory.

If you're used to taking home a weekly or biweekly paycheck, the first year or so of managing those fluctuations can be difficult. Through good budgeting, an effective marketing strategy (to keep the client pipeline full), and an honest look at your own financial house, you'll find yourself much better prepared to handle the fluctuations that are sure to come your way.

The Basics

Just how much you can expect to earn as a real estate agent depends on a few critical factors:

❑ *How Much Time You Put into the Business:* Part-timers, for example, will generally not make as much as those working the business forty to sixty-plus hours per week.

❑ *The Size of Your Own Networking Circle:* Those agents who have a steady flow of potential buyers and sellers at their fingertips tend to do more deals that those who start from scratch on each new deal.

❑ *Your Effective Use of Technology and Related Tools:* The agent who totes around a laptop with real-time access to the local Multiple Listing Service, for example, can print out comparative market analyses for a potential seller in a flash (compared to the agent who has to go back to the office to do it, then deliver it or fax it to the customers), then use the time saved to sell more.

❑ *Your Broker's Training Program:* Brokers that offer regular training and that work closely with their agents tend to cultivate more successful salespeople.

❑ *Your Broker's Compensation Arrangement:* It ranges from a 50/50 split (of gross commissions) to a 100 percent arrangement, and everything in between. Keep in mind that those brokers that take higher cuts tend to offer more advertising, marketing support, training, and related necessities than the 100 percent companies.

❑ *Your Commitment to the Business:* If you got into real estate to make a quick buck, you'll probably be disappointed. Most of the agents who are earning high annual salaries tend to be those who are thoroughly committed to the business. They're in it for the long haul and realize that it can take years to build a small business into a profitable entity.

Several different organizations track the earnings of real estate agents, so we'll first look at those put out by the U.S. Bureau of Labor Statistics (BLS). These numbers are usually considered low by industry standards, but they will give you a good idea of the various earnings levels of the nation's residential agents. According to the BLS, the median annual earnings of salaried real estate agents, including commissions, were $30,930 in 2002, with the middle 50 percent earning between $21,010 and $52,860 a year. The lowest 10 percent earned less than $15,480, and the highest 10 percent earned more than $83,780.

The National Association of Realtors' 2003 *Member Profile* paints a rosier picture. Having polled a high percentage of its nearly 1 million nationwide members, the group found that in 2002 the typical agent's median gross personal income was up more than 10 percent over 2000, to $52,200 per year. That means half of agents make less than that amount, and half make more. NAR also reported that agent expenses were holding steady, and that members were keeping more money in their pockets thanks to higher incomes of about $6,900 annually before expenses (these include marketing, administrative services, technology, and other costs of doing business).

With inflation factored in, NAR reports that the expense side is virtually unchanged for the typical practitioner. Of that $6,900, personal marketing takes the biggest bite out of practitioners' income—a median of $1,200. The household income of real estate professionals remains well above that for the country as a whole. Practitioner households earned a median $100,400, about 140 percent higher than U.S. household median income in 2002 of $42,409.

Residential real estate continues to be dominated by independent contractors earning a commission split. Almost 75 percent of practitioners earn a commission split compared with 20 percent earning 100 percent commissions. A few practitioners earn a mix of commissions and salary or profit sharing, or just salary.

In real estate, the BLS says income usually increases as an agent gains experience, but individual ability, economic conditions, and the type and location of the property also affect earnings. Sales workers who are active in community organizations and in local real estate associations can broaden their contacts and increase their earnings, according to the BLS. It reports that a beginning agent's earnings often are irregular, because a few weeks or even months may go by without a sale.

As with many other commission jobs, some brokers will allow an agent to draw against future earnings from a special account; the practice is not usual with new employees. This can be a moving target for some new agents, so it's generally advisable to have a six- to twelve-month reserve on hand before getting into the business. If you begin collecting checks before that reserve runs out, all the better. If you don't, at least you know you're covered and able to concentrate on building your business—not wondering how you're going to pay your bills—during that first year in business.

Hurdling Challenges

Ask any real estate expert what the average real estate agent's biggest challenge is, and the answer will probably be, "sustaining himself from the time he closes the sale until he gets paid." The average sale can take forty-five to sixty days, although it varies from deal to deal. After helping with the negotiations and purchase agreement, the listing and/or selling agent will perform these and other important tasks:

- ❏ Coordinating inspections and other events
- ❏ Fielding calls and answering questions from buyer or seller (depending on which one the agent is representing)

❑ Keeping tabs on the mortgage lending process to be sure it's on track

❑ Documenting all activities related to the sale

❑ Managing the necessary disclosures and related paperwork

❑ Arranging for mold, asbestos, roof, or other inspections

❑ Coordinating with escrow to be sure it is opened in a timely fashion

❑ Verifying with the escrow holder that the deposit was placed in escrow and that funds are sufficient

❑ Reviewing escrow documents with seller

❑ Making arrangements to have all utilities on and operating during the entire escrow period (if property is vacant)

❑ Making arrangements to meet buyer and/or the cooperating agent at all requested inspections

❑ Reviewing and discussing with seller any requested repairs by buyer

❑ Meeting with the appraiser

❑ Coordinating any other items that need to be completed prior to close of escrow

❑ Reviewing closing statements with seller and/or buyer

❑ Making arrangements for buyer to receive keys to the property

❑ Ensuring that all parties know the closing dates, times, and location

As you work your way down this list, you'll keep your eye on the prize: that commission check that comes your way on closing day. For agents, all roads lead to that short period of time at the title company or attorney's office when the loan documents are signed and checks are cut for those service providers who worked on the deal, including you. To avoid living "commission check to commission check," you'll want to make sure your own client pipeline is filled enough to keep those checks coming in on a regular basis. This also ensures that closing delays on certain deals don't impact your finances too severely, as such delays are fairly common in the real estate industry.

There are other ways to ride out the highs and lows of commission life, and they circle back to treating your business like a business (see chapter 8). A line of credit from a local bank, for example, can help even out the fluctuations by providing a financial cushion when times are lean.

When applying for business loans and/or lines of credit, you'll probably be asked to personally guarantee the repayment (particularly if you're new to the business), and the total amount will be based on a percentage of your company's annual sales. If you expect $50,000 in revenues for the upcoming year, then the bank will probably be willing to lend you $5,000 to $10,000 on a line of credit to use as needed. Check with banks in your area for specific details on what programs they offer.

Budgeting is also critical for real estate agents, as is investing for your future (see chapter 9) and being able to meet your own financial obligations while you help clients either sell their homes or purchase new dwellings. Don't neglect your own needs during the process. Be sure to pay yourself an adequate compensation (from each month's commission checks) that covers not only those financial obligations, but also provides adequate money to live on for the month. Here's how to make that happen, no matter what your stage of the game is:

❏ *Brand-New Agent:* Expect to live off your own personal savings, line of credit, or other resource for the first six months. If a sale comes sooner, all the better. When that first check does come in, use this formula to create a healthy balance between your own needs and those of your business. Let's say it was a $3,750 commission check (based on the sale of a $250,000 home, split with the cooperating broker and split 50/50 with your own broker).

○ First, deposit $2,000 to your personal bank account, for living and personal expenses and savings.

○ Then, set aside 20 percent for taxes, or $750 (adjust according to your tax bracket).

○ Last, reserve the remaining $1,000 to either pay off business expenses you've incurred during the last month or retain that money for future business use.

❏ *Existing Agent:* Commission checks aren't new to you, but for some reason you just can't seem to manage the fluctuations associated with your commission-only sales job. If this describes you, try taking that next $5,000 commission check and dividing it up like this:

○ $2,500 to pay your own bills and expenses, and to cover your lifestyle needs.

○ $1,250 to set aside for taxes (based on a 25 percent tax bracket, assuming that an existing agent has higher income than a brand-new agent).

○ $1,000 to pay off business expenses incurred in the last month, such as MLS or Realtor association dues.

○ $250 reserved in a business account for future use, such as rent on a bigger office.

These formulas are not set in stone and are both based on the assumption that you know exactly how much money you need each month not only to live comfortably but also to run your business. If you don't have a handle on this aspect of your career yet, please refer to chapter 2 for an in-depth look at the components that make up your monthly budget and how to adequately cover them, even if you're just starting out in the business. Getting this down on paper (or computer, via a program like Microsoft Money or Quicken) and knowing what your monthly expenditures are (both personally and professionally) will provide yet another tool for managing a fluctuating income.

Filling the Pipeline

Perhaps the most valuable asset you have on your side in the fluctuating income challenge is your ability to meet people and turn them into customers. After all, with a full client pipeline, the odds are good that your checks will be more frequent and fatter. So although fluctuations are typical from time to time, it doesn't necessarily mean that you're going to spend the next twenty years of your life wondering where your next paycheck is going to come from.

Lori Arnold says the key is to plan for the long-term, instead of just working on one paycheck at a time. Just like a small-business owner wouldn't serve one client from start to finish, then go in search for another, the agent shouldn't put all of his time and energy into closing one deal before moving on to the next one. Look beyond today, and realize that in order to keep your income as steady as it can be, you'll need access to a regular supply of:

❑ Potential buyers who are looking to purchase new homes now
❑ Potential buyers who may be ready to buy within the next three to twelve months
❑ Home owners who are ready to sell their homes now
❑ Home owners who are ready to sell within the next three to twelve months

If all four categories are covered (some clients may not fit perfectly, such as the buyer who is ready to purchase in sixty days, but this gives you a general idea), you'll be assured a steady flow of business possibilities.

How you divide up your daily activities is equally as important, since the social nature of the real estate profession can find you bogged down by tasks that don't generate income. Floor time, during which you man the office phones for potential clients, can be very productive, for example. Time spent chatting by the coffeepot waiting for that phone to ring, however, can be better spent on marketing and advertising activities, calling friends and family to remind them that you're there to help if they want to buy or sell, or updating your Web site to reflect updated listings and information.

At Coldwell Banker Apex, both new and existing agents are advised to divide their time between focusing on current clients (in the interest of generating referral business from them), handling their active listings and/or pending contracts, and generating new business by reaching out to prospective buyers and sellers. "Divide your day or week into three equal parts, and be sure to put adequate time into these three different activities," Arnold says. "The agents that do this find that they get their incomes on a more even keel."

Taking the "thirds" approach ensures that you're not only working the business that's in front of you at the moment, but that you're also cultivating existing relationships and building new ones all the time. Doing so virtually ensures that you'll be both lining up commission checks for the next few months as well as setting yourself up for longer-term success, since all of your clients will not be ready to buy or sell at the same time. That person you met at the chamber of commerce meeting last week who mentioned that she is moving out of state in six months, for example, is actually a very warm lead that in six month's time could turn into a hot prospect.

"Too many agents stop prospecting while in the middle of a transaction, and are then forced to start all over again thirty to sixty days later when the deal closes," says Arnold. "This is not a good approach, and it's what leads to major income fluctuations that can eventually lead to failure. On the other hand, those agents who focus on all three aspects of their business gain stability, and avoid the stress of having to deal with the ups and downs of working on commission."

Yet another way to keep such stressors at bay is by keeping some money in reserve, for the lean times. This isn't always easy for newer agents, but there's really no excuse for those entrenched agents to not sock away some money from each check for a rainy day. If you need to open a separate account and deposit $500 from each check into it, go for it. Money market accounts—which pay slightly higher interest rates than regular savings accounts—are a good option. Whatever investment vehicle you choose, the key is to create a cushion on which to fall back should you ever need to go more than two to four weeks without a commission check.

Prospecting, Prospecting, Prospecting

A real estate agent's income will fluctuate in direct proportion to how well she prospects, plain and simple. That means that if an agent slacks off on finding new customers, generating referrals, or cultivating her existing customer base, she'll definitely feel it in the pocketbook. "Agents need to have consistency about their work habits," says David Fletcher of Agents Boot Camp. "They can't back off just because they've had a few sales, nor should they go into panic mode if they haven't made a few sales."

To strike that balance between "making enough" sales

and not entering panic mode, you'll need to schedule regular customer-generation activities. Here are some of the best prospecting strategies to add to your own daily checklist:

- ❏ Farming, or selecting a specific neighborhood, community, or "farm area" to market yourself and your services to on a regular basis
- ❏ Direct mail pieces (Just Sold, Just Listed, etc.)
- ❏ Internet and Web site advertising
- ❏ Using online lead-generation systems like HouseHunt.com or HomeGain.com
- ❏ Newspaper and magazine advertising
- ❏ "Warm calling" potential customers with whom you've had prior contact
- ❏ Calling For Sale By Owner (FSBO) listings
- ❏ Contacting expired or cancelled listings from the local MLS
- ❏ Reaching out to anyone else in your own network who may be ready to buy or sell in the next one to twelve months
- ❏ Asking past clients for two to three of their friends, family, or colleagues who may need an agent now or in the near future

You'll no doubt figure out more creative ways to find customers as you move through your career, but no matter the method the key is to keep doing it on a daily basis, even if you feel that you're busy enough. As with any business, it's the marketing and advertising activities that get shelved first when business is good.

To keep the momentum going in your own business, and avoid future panic attacks, be sure to stay current on your prospecting at all times. This alone will play a key role in just how many ups and downs your income will experience throughout a year's time. (To learn more about setting goals and objectives that fit with your own prospecting needs, please refer to chapter 4.)

Once you've established a prospecting plan, you'll want to keep close track of just how well those activities are paying off for your business. For example:

❏ If you're a **new agent** and you've spent two hours on the phone each day contacting FSBOs and expired listings but haven't gotten a listing of your own in the last ninety days, then it's pretty clear it's time to tweak your prospecting activities to include more productive strategies. You may, for example, want to instead select a specific farm area of about 200 homes and begin sending direct mail to them, highlighting your expertise in that area and willingness to provide home owners with a free comparative market analysis (CMA) during the next thirty days.

❏ If you're an **existing agent** in search of better results from your prospecting, create a chart (on paper or on a computer) that categorizes your activities, how much time spent on each, and number of sales or listings that have come as a result of that prospecting. If one certain area isn't producing results (say, calling potential customers with whom you already have a nonbusiness relationship), it's probably time to spend less time on it and instead invest in an online lead-generation membership or expand your network by joining a local business group.

Improving Market Knowledge

Just how well you know your own market can also play a role in your financial success as an agent. Through basic market research and knowledge, you can dig pretty deeply into your market's statistics to figure out just how many homes are sold annually compared with the total number of homes, and estimate what percentage of that market you'll be able to tap as a residential agent.

"I'm often shocked at how naïve agents are about this," says Greg Herder. "They don't even look at the basic turnover rates." Nationwide, for example, there are roughly 130 million family homes and condominiums. In 2003, about 6 million residential transactions were recorded nationally, which would translate into a 4.8 percent annual turnover rate. Similar information is available at the local level from either your Realtor association or MLS, and can be invaluable when trying to figure out how to best spend your prospecting time. Here's an example that both new and existing agents can use:

- ❑ *Size of the Farm Area:* 1,000 homes (fill in the number of homes in your targeted farm area)
- ❑ *Turnover Rate:* 5 percent (adjust this percentage to coincide with the appropriate percentage for your own region)
- ❑ *Number of Homes That Will Sell in That Specific Area Every Year:* 50 homes

In this example, the agent with the powerful marketing program will probably capture about 50 percent of that market, resulting in 25 sales annually. This is a good frame of reference for any agent, particularly the one who wants to close 100 transactions annually and realizes that to do this, she must quadruple the size of her farm area. "Most agents aren't thinking about this," says Herder. "I know agents who have a farm area of 150 homes with a turnover of 3 percent, or five homes a year. That person would need 100 percent market share to even have a chance of surviving as an agent."

You'll also want to factor in market conditions when selecting farm areas, since real estate's cyclical nature can distort that turnover rate from year to year. If the area is too small by the standards outlined above, for example, a slightly depressed real estate market for twelve to twenty-four months will certainly wreak havoc on your income. Competition is another important consideration, since going head-to-head with an agent who has dominated a particular farm area for years could result in depressing results.

"You really don't want to take on a dominant agent in his own marketplace," says Herder. "Too often, new and growing agents will target an area where another agent is experiencing great success, without doing the market research to find out what chance they have of really penetrating that market."

If you're an existing agent whose sales are growing at 5 to 10 percent (or higher) annually, you'll want to step back and look at the key issues mentioned above, such as:

❏ Putting time every day into prospecting for new buyers and sellers
❏ Thoroughly examining your market, including home-turnover statistics
❏ Using those statistics to determine if your current farm area is adequate, or if it needs to be expanded or replaced
❏ Checking out the competition in your marketplace, particularly in your farm area
❏ Asking yourself: Is there something else that might be eroding my client base?

"If you're stagnating, then you definitely need to tweak your plan," says Herder. "There should be a steady, upward trend in an agent's real estate sales based on natural client-generation tools, such as referrals." And although referrals are a great source of business, they shouldn't be your only revenue stream. To pump up sales, achieve your financial goals, and avoid income fluctuations, you must also feed your client pipeline with new marketing efforts.

Getting Organized

If there's one thing CPA Rob Johanson notices about most real estate agents, it's that they usually need help getting organized. An adviser affiliate with NBS Financial Services in Westlake Village, California, Johanson holds a real estate license himself and often works with agents who are trying to get a handle on their finances. When they come to him, those agents usually lack a separate business account, for example, and are remiss when it comes to documenting business expenses.

"One of the first steps agents should take in getting their finances on track is to open a business bank account, and not operate out of their personal accounts," says Johanson. "If they ever were to be audited, this separates their personal activity and helps to avoid exposing that to unwanted review." It also assists persons who are just starting out in a business to establish the bona fide nature of their activity. This can be important when a start-up net operating loss is encountered.

Going a step further, a dedicated business credit card is another good way to separate business from personal, as are the various loans or lines of credit available to today's business owners. Johanson also suggests a home equity line of credit, which can help even out the fluctuations associated with working in a cyclical business, dependent on commissions. Since

ASKING FOR HELP

Just like the owner of a small manufacturing business has access to companies that will buy her accounts receivables, then pay a percentage to that company (which in turn collects the receivables), real estate agents can tap the services of companies that will purchase their future commissions. One of those companies, for example, is Commission Connection (www.commissionconnection.com), a Greenville, South Carolina–based company that helps agents nationwide manage their cash flow.

In business since 1997, the company offers services that assist agents and brokers with cash flow needs when business expenses arise prior to the settlement and the payment of a commission. In months where expenses outweigh commission income, for example, the service enables agents and brokers to accelerate the payment of commissions under contract to cover the expenses.

It works like this: The agent or broker selling the account receivable receives money from the business buying the account. When the account receivable matures, the buyer of the account receivable is then paid. The service basically bridges the gap between home sale, and the fifteen- to ninety-day period before payment arrives at the closing table.

The fee for the service is a small percentage of the commission and is tax deductible if used for business expenses. According to the company, which calls the service "accelerated commission," the fee is 8 percent of the agent's portion of the commission for a thirty-day settlement, 10 percent for a sixty-day settlement, or 12 percent for a ninety-day settlement. The minimum is $150, and a $49 processing fee is added to each accelerated commission service. The total fee is deducted from the agent's commission check at closing.

Companies that pay advance commissions have slightly different policies. Some ask the broker in charge to pay the company at closing, other companies are paid by the closing agent. Some companies will ask the agent to submit more paperwork than others to apply for an account or when requesting an advance. Here's a list of the companies that currently offer commission factoring to agents and brokers:

Agent's Equity Inc.
Web site: www.agentsequity.com
Phone: (800) 331-9756
1867 Yonge Street
Suite 1001
Toronto, Ontario M4S 1Y5

Commission Connection
Web site: www.commissionconnection.com
Phone: (800) 486-1025
500 East North Street, Suite F
Greenville, SC 29601

Commission Express
Web site: www.commissionexpress.com
Phone: (703) 560-5500
8306 Professional Hill Drive
Fairfax, VA 22031

eCommission
Web site: www.ecommission.com
Phone: (877) 882-4368
5914 West Courtyard Drive
Suite 320
Austin, TX 78730

Before conducting business with a commission-factoring company, take the time to thoroughly investigate the company and its practices. Ask the companies for both current and past referrals, then call the agents directly to find out how well the system worked for them, whether it was worth the fee, and what challenges it posed for them. You'll also want to talk to your broker before taking this step to determine if there is a better way to generate income to fill in during the lean times.

earnings will change from year to year, good tax planning is equally as essential (see chapter 6 for more information) as are investment vehicles like college savings accounts, retirement plans, and insurance policies.

Knowing that these important financial components are in place—and that they're funded by your income—can help you stay on track with both the prospecting and selling side of the real estate business. Although a part-time agent may be able to afford to slack off once in a while to focus on other things, the full-time agent whose retirement accounts and college savings funds are waiting for cash infusions will be more apt to strive for a steady, predictable income.

"You need to be able to normalize your expected income over an entire year, keep track of your earnings, and know exactly where you are financially at any given time," Johanson says. By tracking income on a quarterly and annual basis, for example, you'll be better equipped to make accurate, estimated tax payments that avoid penalties when April 15th rolls around.

Whether you maintain those records on an Excel spreadsheet, financial software application, or even a paper-based system, the key is to create an organized, easy-to-access-and-update method, and you'll soon find yourself much better equipped to deal with any income fluctuations thrown your way.

CHAPTER SIX

Tax Planning and Preparation

''IN THIS WORLD NOTHING

IS CERTAIN BUT DEATH AND TAXES.''

—BENJAMIN FRANKLIN

They say the only things guaranteed in life are death and taxes, and no one knows this better than the average real estate agent. Although they may hang their license on a broker's wall and work in the office on a regular basis, agents truly are the masters of their own domain when it comes to taking care of their tax obligations, tracking expenditures and income, and filing in a timely, accurate manner according to predetermined schedules.

One agent found this out quickly after leaving her information technology job a few years back in search of greener pastures. She found them in residential real estate, a field where she could control her own destiny and have more flexibility. It didn't take long for this now-successful, Florida-based agent to find out just how much she'd taken on by leaving her paycheck behind, particularly when it came to tax management.

"The first year or so, I really did no business or tax planning," says the agent, who, with a partner, sold $10 million in properties in 2003. "The transition from manager to small-business owner wasn't easy."

Although the pair knew they had to put away twenty-five to thirty cents of every dollar earned to cover tax liabilities, she says they still lacked basic tax planning knowledge. As a result, deadlines came as a surprise, as did total tax amounts due for estimated taxes and self-employment tax (which takes a whopping 15.3 percent off of a sole proprietor's bottom line).

"We really didn't have control of the situation," the agent says. "It kind of hit us by surprise because we always *knew* we had to plan, but actually sitting down and planning out a year in advance and putting it on paper was a different story. During the first year or so, everything just kind of hit us after the fact."

After winging it for those first twelve to eighteen months and getting socked with tax liabilities and penalties for not making adequate estimated payments, the agent used her experience in the technology field to develop a number of Microsoft Excel spreadsheets, which are used for budgeting and business planning.

Both she and her partner then incorporated as subchapter S corporations and completely separated their personal finances from their business finances. The final piece of the puzzle was a Quicken program for personal finances and a QuickBooks software program to manage monthly, quarterly, and yearly income and expenses.

"Once we started planning during that second year, it all kind of fell into place," the agent recalls. "We realized that we had to have completely separate business and personal financial plans, and that planning really pays off when it comes to taxes."

Taxing Matters

Faced with a full workload, demanding clients, the need to make a living, and only so many hours in the day to do so, real estate agents tend to get caught off guard when tax time rolls around. Because commission checks are paid in full, with no taxes withheld, agents are largely on their own when it comes to managing their taxes. Poor record keeping is usually the biggest culprit. Busy tracking down listings, spending time with clients, and handling other activities that bring in the money, agents tend to ignore issues like creating potential tax deductions, gathering and recording receipts, budgeting, and tax planning.

In fact, most CPAs who have spent time working with agents will tell you that few agents properly plan their finances, and as a result wind up grappling with the tax system. At the heart of the problem are those agents who don't think of themselves as business owners, and as such don't organize business receipts, keep separate business records, form corporations, or maintain separate checking accounts.

"At the end of the year most agents are disorganized, scrambling around to find receipts and records," says one CPA who works often with agents, and who advises them to completely separate their real estate activities from their personal finances. That means opening a separate checking account and credit card account, and using them only for depositing commission checks and paying out expenses like advertising, overhead, and travel. That way, when April 15th or August 15th rolls around (depending on whether you filed an extension this year or not), you won't have to pore over bank and credit card statements to separate personal and business expenses and income.

You'll also want to get a handle on exactly what is expected of you tax-wise, or risk falling behind and incurring stiff penalties for noncompliance. As a self-employed individual, you may be responsible for completing the following forms. Check with your individual city and state for income and related tax requirements, and follow these IRS filing guidelines for self-employed individuals:

❏ If you are self-employed, a sole proprietor (someone who owns an unincorporated business by yourself), or an independent contractor, you are required to report income and expenses on Schedule C or C-EZ and calculate your earnings that are subject to self-employment tax (which is 15.3 percent). Attach the schedule to your Form 1040 U.S. Individual Income Tax Return.

❏ If you are a member of a partnership that carries on a trade or business, your distributed share of its income or loss from the trade or business is included in your net earnings from self-employment. The partnership must report the business income and expenses on a Form 1065 U.S. Return of Partnership Income, along with a Schedule K-1 showing each partner's net income, and file Schedule SE to report your individual self-employment tax.

❏ If you have employees, you must pay employment taxes, including federal income, Social Security, and Medicare taxes.

❏ Estimated tax is the method used to pay (including self-employment tax) on income not subject to withholding. You generally have to make estimated tax payments if you expect to owe taxes, including self-employment tax, of $1,000 or more when you file your return. Use Form 1040-ES to figure and pay the tax.

Streamlined System

One of the best ways to deal with tax issues is to establish a budget for the entire year, then use those figures to estimate tax liabilities, which are due every quarter year-round. You'll also want to find an accounting system that suits your own work style, which these days typically means a computer-based software system like Quicken, Microsoft Money, or QuickBooks. That way, when you're driving clients around to look at homes, purchasing a small ad in a local newspaper, or writing a check for Internet service, you can enter any expenses incurred (gas, meals, advertising expenses, etc.) in the software program and retain the actual receipt in a regular file.

Judith E. Dacey, a CPA at Lady Lake, Florida–based J. D. Sumter Tax Accountants, Inc., says the *minimum* tax bite is about 25 percent of a real estate agent's net profits, broken down as follows:

❏ 10 percent for income tax
❏ 15.3 percent for Social Security and Medicare tax

The latter is generally considered one of the biggest burdens on sole proprietors, who don't pay employment taxes throughout the year and are therefore expected to pay for Social Security and Medicare through their federal tax payments. Self-employment tax (also known as SE tax) is a Social Security and Medicare tax primarily for individuals who work for themselves. It is similar to the Social Security and Medicare taxes withheld from the pay of most wage earners. You must pay SE tax and file Schedule SE if your net earnings from self-employment are $400 or more in any calendar year. As an agent, you can figure SE tax obligations using IRS Schedule SE (Form 1040) and by referring to IRS Publication 533, *Self-Employment Tax*.

To make sure you're adequately budgeting for these types of tax expenses—not just spending commission checks indiscriminately and coming up empty when tax time comes—you'll need to know exactly what is and isn't deductible in your business. After all, if you don't know what you can write off, and under what conditions, then figuring out how much of the leftover pie is really yours will be nearly impossible.

Realize that certain business expenses may be tax deductible, such as supplies, advertising fees, traveling expenses, and your home office, to a certain percentage. Writing off legitimate expenses is important in reducing your tax liability, but be sure you take only the right percentage of legitimate deductions by consulting with your tax adviser. Keep receipts or proof of any and all deductions you plan to take, and be sure that the costs are indeed business expenses. To be deductible, a business expense must be both ordinary (common and accepted in your field of business) and necessary (helpful and appropriate for your business).

A few of the most common business deductions are:

- ❏ Bad debts
- ❏ Car and truck expenses
- ❏ Depreciation
- ❏ Employee pay
- ❏ Insurance
- ❏ Interest
- ❏ Legal and professional fees
- ❏ Rent
- ❏ Pension plans
- ❏ Taxes (federal, state, local, and foreign)
- ❏ Travel, meals, and entertainment
- ❏ Business use of your home
- ❏ Advertising
- ❏ Education expenses
- ❏ Licenses and regulatory fees
- ❏ Subscriptions to trade or professional journals
- ❏ Utilities

Within each of these deduction categories there are both subcategories and rules that spell out whether particular deductions are indeed legitimate. Since you probably don't have time to look up the validity of every business expense for deduction purposes, the best measure is to develop a process of organizing the receipts on a daily or weekly basis, year-round.

"Never wait until April to plow through the drawer full of unrecognizable receipts," cautions Dacey. "Unless it is an asset like office equipment or furniture, the IRS usually does not care when you paid for an expense during the year, so categorize receipts by type of expense."

If you don't already have a system in place for this, try the very simple brown envelope system. At the start of each year, pull out a dozen 9-inch by 12-inch brown mailing envelopes and label them by type of expense, such as:

❏ Advertising/marketing expenses.

❏ Automobile expenses. (Be sure to also keep a written mileage log detailing your business miles. This can be a separate logbook or a notation on client cards, in a personal digital assistant, or on a desk calendar.)

❏ Books, newspapers, periodicals, and subscriptions.

❏ Dues and fees: MLS, electronic lock boxes (agents pay to subscribe and use these tools on homes they list and sell), and the local Realtor board.

❏ Gifts. (Note: This is currently limited to twenty-five dollars per person or related couple.)

❏ Meals and entertainment. (Note: This type of expense is only 50 percent deductible.)

❏ Miscellaneous (use only when needed, and always notate a detailed description).

❏ Office supplies.

❏ Postage.

❏ Refreshments (100 percent deductible).

❏ Seminars/education.

❏ Telephone. (Note: First line into home is not deductible but extra features may be.)

❏ Tolls and parking fees.
❏ Travel.

At the end of each day, empty your pockets or purse and sort receipts into the appropriate envelope. Be sure to always write the amount on the front of the envelope, so that at the end of the year there's no need to paw through unreadable papers. "Just total the numbers on the front of the envelope and voilà!" says Dacey. "And, the best part is that the expenses are already categorized."

Key Considerations

Estimated tax payments, managing 1099s, and dealing with a constantly evolving tax code are enough to make any business owner squirm. Unfortunately, these are just a few of the key issues that agents grapple with in their quest to become efficient taxpayers. Here's a breakdown of some of the key considerations that you need to be thinking about.

Estimated Tax Payments

If you're accustomed to a regular paycheck and weekly deductions from your gross income, then making estimated tax payments will be by far one of the biggest adjustments you'll make as a real estate agent. One successful real estate agent in Illinois prefers to use customized Microsoft Excel spreadsheets for tax planning and tracking. He developed them himself and uses them to:

❏ Track expenses and plan a yearly budget, based on sales projections.

❏ Adjust the budget when necessary.

❏ Utilize the data to file yearly tax returns and estimate quarterly tax payments.

❏ Base those estimated payments either on 90 percent of the current year's income expectations, 100 percent of last year's income, or 110 percent of last year. (Use the latter if you made over $150,000. This is known as the IRS's safe harbor estimated tax payment.)

❏ Adjust estimated tax payments higher or lower, depending on annual sales level (to avoid the risk of getting hit with a 20 percent penalty for underpayment).

To figure your own estimated tax, you must factor in your expected adjusted gross income, taxable income, taxes, deductions, and credits for the year. When figuring your current year's estimated tax, it may be helpful to use your income, deductions, and credits for the prior year as a starting point. Refer to your federal tax return as a guide, and use IRS Form 1040-ES to figure your estimated tax. Visit the IRS Web site at www.irs.gov and click on "Forms and Publications" to download a copy of the form and the publication that goes with it. The 1040-ES form includes a worksheet to help you figure your estimated tax and when payments are due.

See Table 6-1 to help you determine if you need to make an estimated tax payment (based on when you expect to receive commission checks) and when you'll need to make them in order to avoid a penalty.

Employer Identification Numbers

An employer identification number (EIN) is also known as a federal tax identification number and is used to identify a business entity. Generally, businesses need an EIN, although as a sole

Table 6-1. Determining estimated tax obligations.

If you first have income on which you must pay estimated tax:	Make a payment by:	Make later installments by:
Before April 1	April 15	June 15 September 15 January 15 of next year
After March 31 and before June 1	June 15	September 15 January 15 of next year
After May 31 and before Sept. 1	September 15	January 15 of next year
After August 31	January 15 of next year	(None)

proprietor you can also do business on your own Social Security number. Because of identity theft and other issues, many business owners choose to use EINs, and it may be particularly smart for agents who have to share their tax ID numbers when receiving payments via 1099-MISC forms (see next section).

To figure out if the IRS requires you to have an EIN, take this quiz:

- ❑ Do you have employees?
- ❑ Do you operate your business as a corporation or a partnership?
- ❑ Do you file any employment; excise; or Alcohol, Tobacco, and Firearms tax returns?
- ❑ Do you withhold taxes on income, other than wages, paid to a nonresident alien?
- ❑ Do you have a Keogh plan?
- ❑ Are you involved with any of the following types of organizations?
  - ○ Trusts, except certain grantor-owned revocable trusts, IRAs, or Exempt Organization Business Income Tax Returns
  - ○ Estates
  - ○ Real estate mortgage investment conduits
  - ○ Nonprofit organizations
  - ○ Farmers' cooperatives
  - ○ Plan administrators

If you answered yes to any of these questions, you will need to apply online at www.irs.gov or by calling the IRS's Tele-TIN phone number at 1-800-829-4933.

1099-MISC Forms

Another tax issue that real estate agents face on a year-round basis is the management of 1099-MISC forms. These forms are sent to other real estate agents with whom you split commissions and to whom you've paid referral fees, and vice versa. Copies are sent directly to the IRS, which then reconciles them against your reported income when you file your taxes.

Anytime these 1099 payments exceed $600 in any given year (to a single entity), they must be reported to the IRS, unless the recipient's company is incorporated. That means having the party fill out a W-9 form and reporting that payment to the IRS via the 1099-MISC (and also sending one to the recipient). Should you get audited, you would have to pay a $100 penalty (plus interest) for every 1099 that wasn't reported.

To avoid such penalties, you'll want to retain hard copies of all 1099s received throughout the tax year (which, for most, will run from January 1 to December 31), while also recording them in an electronic file for easy reference. Be sure to note any discrepancies between what you were paid and what the 1099 reflects, as the IRS will quickly inform you if your gross income doesn't match up with the 1099 total that it received for the year.

New Tax Laws

The fact that the tax law is constantly changing can also present challenges. In 2004, for example, the top four income tax rates were lowered, retirement contributions were increased, income phase-outs for IRA deductions increased by $5,000, and the maximum deduction thresholds rose to $4,000 for single taxpayers with adjusted gross incomes (AGIs) of $65,000 or less and married taxpayers with AGIs of $130,000 or less.

New tax laws of particular interest to agents include a change to the Section 179 (Expense Deduction) rule, which now allows businesses to deduct rather than depreciate certain business property in the amount of $100,000 (up from $25,000), and a 2004 change to the standard mileage rate system. For 2004, taxpayers using no more than four vehicles could also begin using the standard mileage rate. Previously, those using more than one vehicle at a time couldn't use the standard rate at all and instead had to track the actual expenses for each vehicle.

Also in 2004 the standard mileage rates for the use of a car (including vans, pickups, or panel trucks) rose to $0.375 a mile for all business miles driven, up from $0.36 a mile in 2003; $0.14 a mile when computing deductible medical or moving expenses, up from $0.12 a mile in 2003; and $0.14 a mile when giving services to a charitable organization. More tax law changes came down the pike in 2004, when the IRS's new marriage penalty relief kicked in, the child tax credit increased to $1,000 (up from $600), and retirement contribution limits increased.

There are various other tax-related issues that affect you as an agent, and in the "Hiring Help" section we'll look at how a good tax adviser—working at a rate of $150 to $250 an hour, on average—can help you stay on top of things, just like you would help a home owner or home buyer navigate the home-sales process.

When and What to File

Knowing which tax forms to file—and when they need to be filed—is an important step in getting a handle on your taxes. Whether you're a new agent or an existing agent who hasn't yet nailed down a good tax management system, you'll want to follow the IRS chart in Table 6-2 to figure out exactly what's expected of you, and on what kind of timeline, throughout the year.

Table 6-2.   IRS filing requirements.

If you are liable for:	Use Form:	Deadline for filing:
Income tax	1040 and Schedule C or C-EZ	15th day of 4th month after end of tax year.
Self-employment tax	Schedule SE	File with Form 1040.
Estimated tax	1040-ES	15th day of 4th, 6th, and 9th months of tax year, and 15th day of 1st month after the end of tax year.
Social Security and Medicare taxes and income tax withholding	941	April 30th, July 31, October 31, and January 31.
	943 (Agriculture Taxes)	See IRS Publication 225.
	8109 (to make deposits)	See IRS Publication 15.
Providing information on Social Security and Medicare taxes and income tax withholding	W-2 (to employee)	January 31.
	W-2 and W-3 (to the Social Security Administration)	Last day of February (March 31 if filing electronically).
Federal Unemployment (FUTA) tax	940 or 940-EZ	January 31.
	8109 (to make deposits)	April 30, July 31, October 31, and January 31, but only if the liability for unpaid tax is more than $100.
Filing information returns for payments to nonemployees and transactions with other persons	See Information Returns	Forms 1099—to the recipient by January 31 and to the IRS by February 28 (March 31 if filing electronically). Other forms—See the General Instructions for Forms 1099, 1098, 5498, and W-2G.
Excise tax	See Excise Taxes	See the instructions to the form.

Partnership taxes	1065	April 15 following the close of the partnership's tax year if its accounting period is the calendar year. Fiscal Year Partnership—15th day of the 4th month following the close of its fiscal year. Provide each partner with Sch. K-1 (Form 1065). See Partnerships.
S-Corporation taxes	1120-S 1120-W (Estimated Taxes—Corporations Only and 8109)	15th day of the 3rd month following the date the corporation's tax year ended as shown at the top of Form 1120S. Calendar year—March 15, 2004. If due date falls on a Saturday, Sunday, or legal holiday, file on the next business day. If the S corporation election was terminated during the tax year, file Form 1120S for the S corporation's short year by the due date (including extensions) of the C corporation's short year return. See S-Corporations.
Corporate taxes	1120 or 1120-A 1120-W (Estimated Taxes—Corporations Only and 8109)	15th day of the 3rd month after the end of its tax year. New corporation filing a short-period return—15th day of the

(continues)

Table 6-2.   (Continued).

If you are liable for:	*Use Form:*	*Deadline for filing:*
		3rd month after the short period ends. Corporation that has dissolved—15th day of the 3rd month after the date it dissolved. See Corporations.
Limited Liability Company (LLC)	Only member of LLC is an individual—LLC income and expenses are reported on Form 1040, Schedule C, E, or F.	See Publication 3402.
	Only member of the LLC is a corporation, income and expenses are reported on the corporation's return, usually Form 1120 or Form 1120S.	
	Most LLCs with more than one member file a partnership return, Form 1065. If you would rather file as a corporation, Form 8832 must be submitted. No Form 8832 is needed if filing as a partnership.	

Hiring Help

Some agents choose to go it alone when it comes to the actual tax preparation, although others swear by the services of a good accountant or tax adviser, who can even help you set up a financial software program. To find one, you'll want to ask other agents who they use (since there are usually a few in any area that work often with real estate agents and brokers), use an online directory like CPAFinder.com (which lists accountants by state and specialty), or check with a local business group for a referral.

When one Illinois real estate agent made the move from a salaried job to full-time agent nine years ago, he grappled with a necessity that sends shivers down most agents' spines: paying estimated tax payments on time, and in the appropriate amounts. Today, he socks away 25 percent of each commission check in a separate checking account, specifically for taxes.

"I pretend that money isn't there, until it's time to make my estimated payments," says the agent, who sold $14.4 million in property in 2003. Come April 15th (a double-whammy day for agents, when the previous year's tax returns and the first estimated payment for the current year are due), he doesn't have to scramble to dig up the funds. Along the way, this agent says one of the best tools that an agent can have is a good accountant who understands the tax challenges that small businesses and independent contractors face.

"No one wants to give money away to an accountant, but you have to look at it like selling a home," he says. "It's like doing it by-owner or with a real estate agent; we as an industry know which choice is the most beneficial for the consumer."

Just how much you'll pay an accountant to handle your taxes depends on where you're located and how much of that person's time that you'll require. Remember that a good tax professional will educate you as well as prepare any necessary returns and reports. Use the following guidelines to determine whether an accountant will pay off for you, and just what you can expect in return for your fees:

❏ For every $4,000 that a real estate agent nets during the year, $1,000 of it goes to the IRS. "That provides a lot of incentive to find a knowledgeable pro to help shrink that cost," says Dacey.

❏ Typically, an expert professional for a self-employed, un-incorporated agent will charge $300 to $500 to prepare a tax return.

❏ In return, the agent should expect to meet in person with the expert, who will answer questions about taxes.

❏ The professional should also be available year-round to answer occasional quick questions free of charge by either phone or e-mail.

❏ Additional assistance, such as calculating estimated tax payments due or tax planning will entail a charge of about $150 to $250 per occurrence.

Whether you decide to hire an accountant or go it alone, you'll want to educate yourself on the major issues affecting small-business people, particularly independent contractors like yourself. A few good tax resources for real estate agents are:

❏ *The IRS Itself:* The Internal Revenue Service has an informative small-business Web site at www.irs.gov/businesses/small/index.html. On the site, you'll find details on these and other topics:

  ○ *Online Classroom:* The IRS's Small-Business/Self-Employed online classroom comprises a series of self-directed workshops on a variety of topics for small-business owners.

  ○ *Employer ID Numbers (EINs):* The resources in this section provide a full explanation about the EIN, also known as a federal tax identification number.

  ○ *Employment Taxes for Small Businesses:* A comprehensive employment tax resource for business owners.

○ *Taxpayer Education and Communication (TEC) Phone Numbers:* The IRS maintains local TEC offices in order to establish relationships with organizations and businesses, and to help educate them on small-business tax issues.

○ *The Latest Tax Changes for Businesses:* A rundown on the latest tax code changes that will affect you as a business owner.

○ *Filing Late and/or Paying Late:* Details on how to handle late returns and tax payments.

○ *Self-Employed Individuals or Independent Contractors:* A community dedicated to providing information related to self-employment. Get the basics on self-employment, filing requirements, your reporting responsibilities as an independent contractor, useful forms and publications, and more.

❏ *Tax Guides:* In November of each year Ernst & Young publishes the *Ernst & Young Tax Saver's Guide*, and every January it releases a new *Ernst & Young Tax Guide.* Both are available in bookstores.

❏ *Accounting Web Sites:* The American Institute of CPAs (AICPA) has a Web site at www.aicpa.org that covers the tax issue from various angles.

❏ *Tax Experts:* Quicken's Small-Business Web site at www.quicken.com/small_business/ spans a wide range of tax topics for small-business owners.

Getting Going

Most experts and agents agree that an electronic method of tracking expenses during the year is the best way to get a handle on your taxes without having to deal with reams and reams

TAX MANAGEMENT STRATEGIES
FOR REAL ESTATE AGENTS

❑ Treat your business like a separate entity by maintaining a checking account and/or credit account dedicated only to business purposes.

❑ Use a software program like QuickBooks, Quicken, or Excel to track income and expenses throughout the year.

❑ Record all business expenses by entering them into your accounting system and maintaining hard copies of the receipts in a file.

❑ Use a year-round budget to keep tabs on where you stand financially. Refer to it often, particularly when your income fluctuates up or down significantly.

❑ Base your estimated payments either on 90 percent of the current year's income expectations, 100 percent of last year's income, or 110 percent of last year if you made over $150,000.

❑ When you split a commission with another agent, or pay out a referral fee, ask the recipient to fill out a W-9 form. Issue 1099-MISC forms to those whom you pay over $600 in any given year.

❑ Set up a retirement account, find out what the upper contribution limits are, and start socking money away for your future, tax free.

❏ Hire a good tax adviser or accountant who understands the real estate business.

❏ Check out a Web site like www.quicken.com, read up on any new tax changes that might affect you, and/or discuss them with your tax adviser.

❏ Instead of ignoring potential tax problems, meet them head-on, deal with them, and move on.

of paper, receipt slips, and other distractions. Simply enter them into your system on a daily or weekly basis, then pull up the information to file your:

❏ Estimated tax payments
❏ Quarterly employment tax returns (for those agents who are incorporated)
❏ Annual federal tax returns
❏ Annual city and state tax returns

Although some agents may still opt for the shoe-box system of maintaining receipts, an electronic system will help you keep everything up-to-date and allow you to get an instant snapshot of your finances at any time, so that you're not scrambling through your car, purse, or basement for receipts and records.

Maintain a diary of expenses, get everything on your computer, and update it as often as possible. And even if you do get behind, remember that rectifying the issue now—rather than later—is always a good idea. Then, use the experience as a lesson for next year and start focusing on year-round tax planning versus last-minute strategies to avoid the same challenges next year.

CHAPTER SEVEN

Personal and Professional Development

―――――――――――――――――

''SETTING A GOAL IS NOT THE MAIN THING.

IT IS DECIDING HOW YOU WILL GO ABOUT

ACHIEVING IT AND STAYING WITH THAT PLAN.''

―TOM LANDRY

Becoming a successful real estate agent takes more than just passing prelicensure and licensing exams, and hanging your license on the wall of a broker's office. In fact, most agents will tell you that unlike a doctor or attorney, the educational challenges are fairly low in real estate. The hard part is parlaying that education into a successful career, and that's where the planning comes in.

You've already learned how to create a business plan and marketing plan, and basically think and act like a business owner by getting a handle on issues like incorporation and taxes. In this chapter, we'll take a look at personal and professional development that will either help you break into the industry, or help propel you to the next level. We'll discuss what it takes to stay on the leading edge while creating an enjoyable work and personal life—not always easy in today's hectic business environment.

In this chapter we'll also look at some of the most popular ways to branch out and grow your business beyond just the solo practitioner. That could mean forming a team, partnering with another agent, hiring help, or outsourcing work to what are known as virtual assistants, who specialize in working with real estate agents. You'll also learn about some of the key designations that agents have after their names, find out how to get them yourself, and learn why they're valuable to agents.

Developing Professionally

Professional development in real estate goes beyond taking the continuing education courses that licensees are required to take every two years. (Individual states have their own requirements, so check with your state real estate commission or department of business for specifics.) There are designations to earn, workshops to attend, audiotapes and CDs to buy, online classes to participate in, and a slew of industry-related publications to pore over—and that's just at the macro level. At your local level, you'll also need to stay up-to-date on market knowledge, consumer preferences, housing trends, and other important aspects of the real estate industry.

What you don't want to do is spend too much time or money on professional development opportunities that won't pay off. Because you're not punching a clock or being closely supervised, it's easy to get thrown off track by a three-day out-of-town seminar, then come back to an empty client pipeline. To avoid wasting time on a conference or seminar, both new and existing agents should:

❏ *Ask past attendees* exactly what they gained from attending the course, online educational offering, or seminar. Find out whether it helped them grow their business, expand their professional knowledge, and/or meet new contacts in the industry. If it did none of those, don't waste your time or money.

❏ *Investigate what topics will be discussed* or imparted during the seminar or course and decide if they cover areas where you need help. For example:

     ○ A new agent would probably benefit from a basic half-day class on how to list properties for sale.

     ○ An existing agent who has been in the business for two years would probably want a more advanced or specific half-day course on how to maximize a contact database to grow sales.

❑ *Check out the Internet* for courses and professional development opportunities, and for feedback on them. Real estate agents are a pretty open group that likes to share the best and worst of its experiences. An online community like Real Talk (http://realtalk.internetcrusade.com/) is a great place to pick up useful tidbits of information on just about anything industry related.

As a real estate agent, you'll be required to take certain continuing education (CE) courses to maintain your license. Each state has different requirements, so check with your local board of Realtors or real estate commission for details. In Florida, for example, real estate brokers and salespersons are required to complete fourteen hours of CE every two years after their first license renewal—and prior to their license expiration date—according to the Florida Real Estate Commission's prescribed CE requirements.

The first three topics of a course generally meet the commission's "core law" requirement, while the remaining topics comprise "specialty education" sections of use by real estate professionals. Agents in all states have a wealth of resources available for satisfying their state's CE requirements. Courses can be taken in the classroom, by correspondence, or online. Local Realtor associations, state Realtor associations, universities, community colleges, and real estate schools all offer the courses for fees that range from free to about twenty dollars, depending on the venue and format.

One school, for example, offers a fourteen-hour CE course for $17.50, which includes an eighty- to one-hundred-page textbook and a thirty-question exam. After studying the book, the agent completes the open-book exam, and the school grades the results. To pass, the student must score 80 percent. The school's president estimates that about 99.5 percent of agents take the CE courses via correspondence, with the percentage of online students on the rise as the format gains in popularity.

Agents can also turn to state and national Realtor conventions to tap the many education sessions given by top industry experts. A good number of the sessions have been approved for CE credit. The best way to find the right course or event is by consulting with other agents and brokers for recommendations. Get your hands on the books or materials that those courses use, and browse through them before signing up. Look for readability, accuracy, thoroughness, and relevance to your business.

CE courses go beyond just fulfilling a requirement. They can also help agents keep up with a constantly changing marketplace where recent developments in laws relating to condominiums, timesharing, building code violations, pool-safety regulations, and federal income taxes are important.

Also key are the disclosure requirements and legal liability associated with polybutylene plumbing pipes, toxic mold, radon, Megan's law, brownfields, lead-based paint, fair housing, financing trends, automated underwriting, valuation, and contracts—not to mention the all-important ethics that NAR and all state real estate regulatory bodies place a high emphasis on. Here are a few great ways to make the most out of the required CE experience and to apply the knowledge you've learned in your own business setting:

❏ Before choosing a course or format, talk to a few agents and brokers to find out which courses and formats they've used in the past, then base your decision on these positive or negative experiences.

- ❏ Instead of taking the cheap and quick way out, opt for a course that has true takeaway value and additional modules like finance or ethics that you can apply to your own business.

- ❏ Know your learning style and choose a format that matches it. Do you learn by the book? Do you prefer an interactive, classroom setting? Would you rather read the course and take the test on your computer?

- ❏ If you're taking a correspondence course, as many agents do, flip through a few of the books to look for readability, accuracy, thoroughness, and relevance to your business.

- ❏ View CE as an opportunity to learn about changes to the license, your state real estate commission's rules, and recent developments, along with other laws relating to real estate.

- ❏ Translate the words that are flat on the course page into three-dimensional strategies by asking yourself: How can I use this in my business? How can I apply this newfound knowledge to my day-to-day routine?

- ❏ While taking the course, look for ways to move the abstract information on that flat page into counseling, listing, and sales presentations.

- ❏ If you're taking CE in a classroom setting, look for an instructor who encourages classroom participation. Many agents learn just as much from the examples and experiences of the group as from the material itself.

- ❏ Come to class ready to focus on the material and contribute to the group discussions. If possible, read the material before the class begins to get a head start.

- ❏ And last, view CE as an opportunity rather than an obligation, and look for tidbits of information and knowledge that you can apply in your own business.

As a real estate professional, it's important to balance professional and personal development with your daily work obligations. Although there are certain courses that you will have to complete to keep your license active, there are only so many hours in a day for the rest. With the proliferation of online learning you may find yourself bombarded with options. Research them carefully, selecting only those that will truly add value to your career, rather than wasting your time on those that sap your finances and time.

Getting Credentialed

As you peruse local listings or newspaper advertisements, you're sure to see a number of credentials and designations following agents' names. The most common of them is the REALTOR® designation ("Realtor" throughout this book), which signifies that the real estate agent, broker, or associate holds an active membership in a local real estate board that is affiliated with the National Association of Realtors. There are about 1 million Realtors nationwide who must adhere to NAR's code of ethics and other guidelines when doing business.

According to NAR, 31 percent of Realtors hold at least one designation awarded from one of the group's affiliated institutes, societies, and councils. The most widely held designations are Graduate, Realtor Institute (GRI); Certified Residential Specialist (CRS); and Accredited Buyer Representative (ABR®). NAR reports a positive relationship between such designations and agent income. In 2002, for example, the typical Realtor holding at least one designation earned $73,100—70.8 percent higher than the median $42,800 income for Realtors without a designation.

Here's a look at some of the most popular designations and

credentials that you may or may not want to pursue as an agent. Before making the commitment to earn any of these credentials, realize that other than the Realtor designation, most experts agree that the average consumer cannot discern between the various acronyms, nor do they shop around for real estate agents based on such credentials. The benefits come in the way of education and knowledge, as well as respect from peers who do understand what it takes to earn these designations.

❏ *Accredited Buyer Representative (ABR):* This designation is awarded to real estate practitioners by NAR's Real Estate Buyer's Agent Council (REBAC). To qualify, agents must meet specified educational and practical experience criteria, including: Successful completion of the two-day ABR® Designation Course and an 80 percent passing grade on the exam. Upon successful completion, agents have three years to complete the other three requirements, which include successful completion of the one approved elective course, documentation verifying five completed transactions in which the agent acted as a buyer representative, and membership in good standing in the Real Estate Buyer's Agent Council and NAR. Learn more at: www .rebac.net.

❏ *Accredited Land Consultant (ALC):* A professional designation made available by NAR's Realtors Land Institute (RLI). The Institute brings together specialists in the sale, management, agribusiness, planning, appraising, acquisition, syndication, and development of land. Its purpose is to establish professional standards, to provide educational experiences for members to assist them in keeping pace with rapid changes in land utilization and prices, and to exert influence in the formulation of public policies affecting farm and land development. Membership is open to anyone who holds membership in a local association of Realtors and who has a desire to increase proficiency, professional standing, and earnings in the field of land-use specialization. Learn more at: www.rliland.com.

❏ *Certified International Property Specialist (CIPS):* The CIPS network is composed of 1,500 real estate professionals from fifty countries who deal in all types of real estate, but who are focused specifically on the international market. Learn more at: www.realtor.org/cipshome.nsf/pages/education.

❏ *Certified Property Manager (CPM):* A professional designation made available by NAR's Institute of Real Estate Management (IREM). The Institute has dedicated itself to developing professionalism in the field of property management by setting standards of performance, experience, and ethics, and by making available educational courses and publications to assist individuals and Realtors in gaining skills essential to quality performance in this field. Learn more at: www.irem.org.

❏ *Certified Real Estate Brokerage Manager (CRB):* Recognized industry-wide as the measure of success in brokerage and real estate business management, this designation is awarded by the Council of Real Estate Brokerage Managers to Realtors who have completed the group's advanced educational and professional requirements. The CRB Designation Program provides credit for management experience, higher education, and previously earned NAR designations, and additional credits can be earned through the CRB's management education programs delivered live or by self-study on CD-ROM. Learn more at: www.crb.com.

❏ *Certified Residential Specialist (CRS):* This is a professional designation that is available through the Council of Residential Specialists, which offers a wide range of courses, sales aids, computer software, and publications for those engaged in residential sales and real estate brokerage management. By providing practical education for its members and working with them to establish sound and ethical practices, the CRS seeks to promote the professional standing of real estate agents. Learn more at: www.crs.com.

❏ *Graduate, Realtor Institute (GRI):* This is a ninety-hour, nationally recognized designation course. Agents earn the GRI designation online or in a classroom setting. The courses are divided into three tracts: GRI One (real estate transactions, finding listings, pricing listings to sell); GRI Two (writing a business plan, loan closings, professional standards); and GRI Three (brokerage management, investing in real estate, and single-family property management). Learn more at: www.realtor.org/griclear.nsf.

❏ *Performance Management Network (PMN):* A newer Realtor designation created to enhance agents' real-world skills. This designation focuses on the idea that in order to enhance your business, you must enhance yourself. The curriculum is driven by the following topics: negotiating strategies and tactics, networking and referrals, business planning and systems, personal performance management, and cultural differences in buying and selling. Learn more at: www.wcr.org.

❏ *REALTOR e-PRO®:* A training program presented entirely online to certify real estate agents and brokers as Internet Professionals. Through the course, agents also learn how to leverage their people skills into doing more business on the Internet. Learn more at: www.epronar.com.

Growing Your Business

There comes a time in every good agent's life when there are simply not enough hours in the day to do all of the business that comes your way. It's every new agent's dream scenario, but it can quickly turn into a nightmare for the existing agent who suddenly finds himself working 24/7, trying to close deals, show homes, create marketing materials, and submit listing materials to the MLS.

To keep your business growing, you have several ways to alleviate the stress and strive for higher sales and more closed transactions. Here's a look at the five basic choices, and the pros and cons of each:

1. Hire a part- or full-time licensed assistant.
   - ❑ Pro: You can almost immediately begin to unload all tasks (even those related to the real estate transaction) to this new person.
   - ❑ Con: You become an employer and manager, and you may be training your next competitor.
2. Hire a part- or full-time unlicensed assistant.
   - ❑ Pro: The new person can handle all of your administrative tasks, such as taking phone calls, checking e-mail, and filing.
   - ❑ Con: You become an employer and manager, and in most states this employee cannot handle any tasks directly related to the real estate transaction.
3. Pair up with another agent in your office.
   - ❑ Pro: If the match works well, the two of you can share all aspects of your workloads, and even cover for each other when one person is sick or on vacation.
   - ❑ Con: You'll need to work out an amicable compensation split when sharing deals, and you may not always find the best match on the first try.
4. Form a team.
   - ❑ Pro: You can spread the work among your team, which would likely be made up of a buyer specialist,

listing specialist, transaction coordinator, and administrative assistant.

❑ Con: Though a popular choice for today's agents, teams take time and care to cultivate and grow. Finding the right team members can be a challenge, but when you hit on the right mix you're sure to realize higher sales and overall success.

5. Outsource some of the work to a virtual assistant (either on-site or off-site).

❑ Pro: You're not an employer, since these professionals operate as independent contractors on a 1099 basis.

❑ Con: Since this person probably won't work in your office, he will work under little supervision. Also, virtual assistants without specific real estate training may lack the industry knowledge needed to perform work quickly and accurately.

Here are three real-life examples of how real estate agents have successfully grown their businesses by taking three different paths. Use this information to determine which option will work best for your own situation.

CASE STUDY #1: HIRING AN UNLICENSED ASSISTANT

As a single mother with a blossoming real estate career, one agent was at the end of her rope just two years ago. Determined to handle it all on her own, she was just two years into her new role as an agent—having run her own real estate company for five years prior—when her work time started cutting into the time she wanted to spend with her twelve-year-old son.

"I was stretching my work later and later into the evening, and I really didn't want to do that to my son," she says. "I was

returning calls at all hours and carrying way too many tasks over to the next day."

The positive side, of course, was that her real estate business was booming—so much so that she was financially secure enough to hire someone to ease that time crunch. Before searching for the right person, she first jotted down a list of everything she was doing that could reasonably be delegated, like putting up for-sale signs, following up on showings, getting keys made, and taking photographs.

The agent then created a flowchart and aptly named it her "assistant's duty checklist." She then set out to find the right person to handle those duties. After considering a few agents who—despite their low sales—were licensed and knowledgeable about the business, she landed on what she calls the perfect choice: her father.

"My broker mentioned that some of the female agents were working with their spouses, but I didn't have one of those," she says. "It occurred to me, however, that my father had just retired and was trying to keep himself busy, so I hired him as my assistant."

The agent spent a few months showing dad the ropes of the real estate business and teaching him some computer basics. Together, the pair sold just under $7 million in properties in 2003, or $1 million more than the year prior. This year, they're hoping for $8 million, now that the new addition—who is not a licensed real estate agent—has become more acclimated to the business.

"What he lacks in computer skills and real estate knowledge he more than made up for in understanding and putting up with me," says the agent. "The extra million dollars in sales was significant, but even more important is the fact that I can now go home at six o'clock every night. I am a new woman *because I've been able to exceed my production level without paying for it in stress or lack of time with my son."*

CASE STUDY #2: FORMING A TEAM

One real estate agent's eight-person team of licensed Realtors pooled their efforts to close 250 transactions in 2003, up from the fifty a year that he closed while working on his own.

The agent assembled the team about seven years ago after noticing that the area's housing market was heating up and recognizing that expanding into different areas of the business—such as buyer's agents, of which the team now has three—would be impossible for a single agent. "I also saw an opportunity to free myself up and become more available," he says.

Of course, working with eight different people to coordinate 250 transactions a year is much different from handling fifty by yourself. According to this agent, communication is the biggest challenge. "Sometimes, a client will speak with one of my team members and assume that I'll know what's going on with that particular issue," he says. To avoid communication gaps, he says the eight members hold regular team meetings and "keep close tabs on each other.

"Everyone is pretty good at recognizing whether I need to know something, but I also just have to pay attention and know when something demands my personal attention," he says, adding that the team also "e-mails one another like crazy" and relies on cell phones to keep those lines of communication open.

Another agent formed a three-person team after twenty-two years of managing a frenzied pace in the real estate industry. He took a step back in 2001 and realized that he could no longer grow his business and live a balanced life with the help of one administrative assistant. "I was running around like a crazy person," he says. "I was doing enough business, but I just couldn't do any more."

And with that, the agent set out to form a team that today comprises one unlicensed administrative assistant, Chally, and his Realtor partner, who works primarily as a buyer's agent. Together, the trio closed 120 transaction sides in 2003, compared to eighty in 2000.

Delegating tasks was fairly easy for the agent, mainly because he was so overloaded at the time and ready for help with everything from answering incoming phone calls from buyers to arranging showings and writing up purchase contracts. Along with the increased business, he says his team has also brought him peace of mind in an industry where the phrases flexible schedule *and* real estate *are rarely synonymous.*

"It's like having multiple bosses, since every time a client signs a contract that person becomes a new 'boss' for the agent," he says. "Things can get pretty hurried and out of control, particularly when you try to take a day off, but thanks to my team I no longer feel like I'm hostage to my business."

CASE STUDY #3: OUTSOURCING WORK TO A VIRTUAL ASSISTANT

It wasn't that long ago that one real estate agent was spending his entire workday dealing with pending transactions. Although he had a full-time, on-site assistant handling administrative and marketing tasks, the agent was still bogged down by the time-intensive transaction management process.

"We were trying to do everything here, and it kind of stunted my growth," says the agent, who heard about a virtual assis-

tant (VA) who was already coordinating transactions for other agents, and decided to check it out. Rather than hire a full-time employee, he worked out an arrangement with the VA, who charges about thirty to fifty dollars an hour (depending on the scope of the work) for ten to twenty hours of work every week.

"Once a file goes into pending status, she takes it and runs with it until we're ready to close," says the agent, who estimates that his business has grown by 25 to 30 percent as a result of outsourcing transaction management duties. "We've grown because I'm no longer tied down to the filing cabinet next to my desk."

Another agent has also found success using VAs. Unless a task needs "legs," she'll outsource it to one of her four VAs. She also employs an on-site assistant to handle office duties but relies on the VAs to handle the rest of the tasks, with the help of technology solutions like Mangomind (an online collaboration tool) and SettlementRoom (where closing paperwork is handled in an online setting).

The agent says the online platform, through which team members can post documents for review by all parties, allows for collaboration with minimal phone calls and faxes. She estimates that the VAs save her about $150,000 a year, based on the fact that they maintain their own work spaces, use their own equipment, and handle their own tax obligations.

Most important, they don't get paid when there isn't any work to do. "You use them and pay them only when you need them," she adds. "It's great."

One Massachusetts real estate agent with twenty-eight years of experience in the business has, over time, mastered

EIGHT TEAM-BUILDING TIPS

1. Look for an assistant, partner, or team member whose strengths and weaknesses complement your own.

2. Check with your individual company's guidelines and state real estate commission's rules for hiring assistants or forming teams before making any decisions about expanding your business.

3. When pairing up with other agents or unlicensed assistants, look not only at their real estate skills and knowledge, but also at their communication and people skills.

4. Talk to your broker or office manager for suggestions on finding a partner, team, or assistant who will be most compatible with your own skills.

5. Work out an amicable pay scale or compensation plan that works for everyone involved. A team of three agents, for example, may opt to split expenses and commissions three ways.

6. Start out slowly by delegating time-consuming tasks like database management and follow-up calls that steal your time away from working directly with home buyers and sellers.

7. Once you find the right person or team members, set your sights not only on increasing your sales, but also on freeing up your own personal time.

8. Don't let one bad choice of assistants or partners ruin your chances of multiplying your success. If at first you don't succeed, try, try again!

the art of building a successful business without sacrificing his personal life. In 2003, he closed 100 transactions, bringing in $20 million on an average sales price of $200,000. Rewind back to the 1980s, however, and he says he was just another agent who was burning the candle at both ends. That was, until he realized that his children and spouse needed him just as much as his business did, if not more.

"I found out a long time ago that I had to plan my personal life first and my business life second," says the agent, who is proud to say he never missed a parent-teacher conference, soccer game, or dance recital.

Setting those priorities also helped his business, which has grown steadily over the last two decades and today comprises eight offices and 220 agents. "The formula is simple: The more time you schedule—both personal and business—the more money you will make," he says. "The balance plays a key factor in that success because when you're working, you will really work; and when you're playing, you will really play."

Jeff Lasky, a twenty-year real estate veteran who is currently in a management position at MAP MLS in Palatine, Illinois, says setting priorities is especially important in the real estate industry, where seemingly legitimate tasks can take all day to complete. Without a boss looking over your shoulder, urging you on, you can easily allocate too much time to those obligations that do little to advance your career.

"I've seen a lot of agents spend too much time on stuff that takes them away from what they really need to be doing: lead generation and business development," says Lasky. "In this business, the most successful agents have a razor-sharp focus on three or four 'big rocks,' and they work on those, in priority order. The other tasks have to get done too, but they can usually be handled later, after the most important tasks are off your desk."

THE RIGHT CHOICE?

Here are some clues that a virtual assistant might be the right solution for your growing real estate business:

❏ You need help on a per-project basis that doesn't warrant a full- or part-time staff member.

❏ You need more time to sell property.

❏ You aren't focusing on your core competencies (sales, consultations, investments, etc.).

❏ You have limited space available in your office for additional staff members.

❏ You are totally overwhelmed in your business and can't keep up with the details.

❏ You're willing to delegate and give up some control over noncore tasks to an off-site assistant.

❏ You're a people person who doesn't like hanging around the office doing paperwork.

❏ You're a brand-new agent who has experienced early success and is in need of assistance but not ready to hire full-time help.

❏ You don't have the time to handle all of the necessary marketing tasks that need to be done.

❏ You're not technology oriented and would rather have someone else handle tasks like up-dating accounting software and creating virtual tours.

❏ You know what needs to be done, but you just don't have time to do it all.

❏ After months of training your last on-site assistant, he or she became your competitor.

Setting Priorities

If you haven't realized it yet, setting priorities is absolutely critical when you're operating as a small-business person in a commission-based environment. Without preset parameters to help you maximize your time, it's very easy to get caught up in day-to-day tasks that take up too much of your time while not producing enough income. In real estate, for example, the following activities tend to consume an agent's time, yet aren't always the most profitable use of time:

❏ Socializing with other agents and brokers in your office over coffee

❏ Socializing with other agents and brokers from outside offices

❏ Attending association and trade meetings that may not have a direct impact on your business

❏ Giving advice to home owners and home buyers who have no intention of using your services in exchange for a fee

❑ Browsing the Internet and/or MLS systems in search of area information, new and expired listings, or other chance opportunities

Granted, some of these activities can produce business, but only if used in moderation. If you don't have a way of outsourcing some of the more mundane tasks to another individual, you'll definitely want to start setting both personal and business priorities. In return, you can truly expect to make the best use of your time while still being able to lead a satisfying life outside of work.

EFFECTIVE TIME MANAGEMENT TACTICS FOR REAL ESTATE AGENTS

❏ Outsource tasks that you don't have the time and/or expertise to complete.

❏ Finish projects early to reduce deadline stress and lighten your own workload.

❏ Know your own limits, or risk the possibility of burnout. If you're hitting overload, for example, take a few hours off for a walk in the park or a good workout. Have lunch with a friend.

❏ Strive for organization by taking time at the end of the workday to get ready for the next day.

❏ Use an agenda (either electronic or written down) and follow it, crossing off tasks as you complete them.

❏ Divide up your time by deciding just how much to spend on business development, personal needs, and family/friend obligations.

❏ Allow for flexibility in your schedule and surround yourself with reliable friends, family, and coworkers who can help out in the time of need.

❏ Make it clear to clients that you are not an around-the-clock agent, but that you are indeed a capable and competent professional who works set hours. (Hint: Print those hours on your business cards for maximum effectiveness.)

Start Now

Assuming that this book has already given you a good idea of how to create a roadmap for your business, develop your professional self, set priorities, and create both marketing and business plans, the best personal development steps you can take right now involve your Palm Pilot or paper-based calendar. Using whatever mechanism works best for you, it's time to:

- ❏ Jot down all of your personal appointments (including gym workouts, gatherings with friends, and family events).
- ❏ Add in all floor time, training sessions, and other broker-related activities that you're asked to partake in.
- ❏ Block out time every day or week for important business tasks like lead generation, farming, and customer follow-up.
- ❏ Then, carve out areas of the day and/or week where business appointments and meetings would fit best.
- ❏ When calls come in for showings, listing appointments, or other obligations, refer to your calendar before saying yes.

Lasky calls this strategy "time blocking" and says that to make it work you'll need to set certain appointments—particularly the personal ones—as "unalterable."

"Many agents will make the time for lead generation, but when something comes up it's usually the family or personal time that suffers as a result," says Lasky. "New agents have an especially hard time blocking out a Saturday afternoon to spend with their kids, then preserving that time when someone calls for a listing appointment. It's very difficult to pass that up."

By establishing boundaries, setting priorities, and laying down the law right now, both new and existing agents will find themselves in much more control of a career that can easily run twenty-four hours a day, seven days a week, if you let it.

Sticking to this routine may be harder than it sounds during your first year or two in business—you'll likely be more focused on getting commission checks than getting to the gym for that aerobics workout on time—but try it anyway. By taking time for yourself, your family, and friends when you can and setting priorities, you'll have a much better handle on the situation. A bonus in implementing these practices will be to avoid the burnout many new and existing agents grapple with on a daily basis.

CHAPTER EIGHT

Treat It Like a Business

''LET OUR ADVANCE WORRYING
BECOME ADVANCE THINKING AND PLANNING.''

—SIR WINSTON CHURCHILL

Just because real estate agents have a desk, on-the-job training, and guidance from a broker or manager, it doesn't mean they can afford to act like employees. "Real estate may feel like a job," says one successful agent, "but it's really anything but." In real estate since 1989, this agent sells about $8 million in properties each year and says she wishes someone had informed her of her small-business owner status a lot earlier in her career.

"This is no sales job," says the agent. "You have to treat it as if you were self-employed, and like you are the CEO of your own company. It took me ten years to realize that I was a business owner, and not just someone who was driving around selling homes." Once she did catch on, she incorporated her business and got a grip on her expenses, instead of spending commission checks freely as they came in.

These days, the agent cuts herself a regular paycheck, pays payroll taxes monthly, allocates a portion of her business's income for estimated tax payments, and tracks expenditures carefully—just like any good business owner would. As a result, she says she has a good handle on her company's revenues and expenditures, knows how profitable her business is, allocates a certain percentage of revenues to marketing, and is much better prepared when tax time rolls around.

Having worked with hundreds of real estate agents over the years, Greg Herder sees more than his fair share of successes and failures. By far, Herder says, the biggest mistake that agents make is that they treat their new career like a job, rather than a business. Unfortunately, since the majority of them work on commissions, that kind of mistake can get pretty costly, pretty quickly.

"Agents know that they're independent contractors, but they still operate as if they had jobs," says Herder. "That kills most agents' chances for success because no matter how many hours they put in, they won't get paid unless they actually perform, and sell homes." The fact that real estate is a time-consuming, all-encompassing type of job doesn't help either. Agents can literally spend all day answering phone calls, driving through neighborhoods, cruising the MLS for new and expired listings, and pressing the flesh with their contact base—all without generating any immediate income.

"So many agents struggle with that mentally, and never quite grasp the fact that just because you put in the time, doesn't mean you're going to make money," says Herder. He advises all agents to create a business plan to avoid getting sidetracked by mundane, day-to-day tasks that don't generate income. "Creating a business plan will significantly increase the odds of succeeding in this business."

Business Sense

The correlation between thinking like a business owner and acting like a real estate agent is clear, but how does one go about adopting that mindset? Start by asking yourself the following twenty pertinent questions that any new entrepreneur should consider before opening up a new business:

1. Am I a hard worker?
2. Am I self-motivated?
3. Am I an optimist and a risk taker, like most successful business owners are?

4. Do I have the self-starter determination to get this business going, and the discipline and dedication to keep it on track?

5. Do I take responsibility for my own actions?

6. Am I a good problem solver?

7. Am I organized?

8. Do I have the stamina and desire to put in long hours?

9. Am I willing to work weekends and evenings, when most home buyers are out looking at houses?

10. Do I consider ethics and honesty to be important ingredients for a successful career in business?

11. Am I usually able to come up with more than one way to solve a problem?

12. Can I live on my savings and/or my partner's income for at least six to twelve months while I build this business?

13. Will my family and friends support my efforts?

14. Am I business savvy, or do I have a colleague or friend who can help me through the critical first few stages of business?

15. Am I prepared to make sacrifices in my family life and take a cut in pay to succeed in business?

16. Am I the kind of person whom nothing can stop once I decide to do something?

17. When I begin a task, do I set clear goals and objectives for myself?

18. When I've done a good job, am I satisfied in knowing personally that the job has been done?

19. After a severe setback in a project, am I able to pick up the pieces and start over again?

20. Do I enjoy working on projects that I know will take a long time to complete successfully?

Don't worry if you didn't answer a resounding yes to every one of these questions, but if you were negative on five or more points, you may want to reconsider the small-business aspect of being a real estate agent. It's truly an entrepreneurial endeavor, particularly for the first two to three years, and a big undertaking that is not for the faint of heart. The sooner you come to grips with this reality, the better off you'll be. That means putting in long hours, operating on a lean and often fluctuating income, striving to find and keep customers, and even spinning your wheels a bit as you figure out what strategies work best so that you ultimately reap the rewards of your sweat equity.

Judith E. Dacey works with real estate agents and brokers, helping them incorporate their companies, manage their taxes, and create overall business success strategies. Dacey says being self-employed requires a 180-degree switch in viewpoint, particularly if the agent hails from a nine-to-five job setting.

"Employees are rewarded for showing up every day, interacting pleasantly with peers and clients, and doing their assigned tasks," says Dacey. "They have little direct stake in the results achieved or concern about net profits or making final management decisions." Agents, on the other hand, are largely responsible for their own success. "Employee behavior will generate only marginal income," Dacey says. "Lack of management perspective can result in long hours, little reward, and burnout."

To avoid such issues in your own real estate career, you'll need to organize your business approach. Start your own organizational journey with these seven easy steps:

1. Start at square one, like any new business owner would. Instead of jumping right into selling homes, spend time

planning, assessing, and researching before "opening your doors."

2. Identify what you're selling, to whom, and how you'll go about doing that. (See chapter 3.)

3. Pick a specialty and stick with it. "No one should be a 'threshold' agent [anyone who walks across the threshold qualifies as a client]," says Dacey. "Just like Starbucks deals only in high-end coffees. Its marketing matches their niche customers, and their environment is specifically designed for the upscale crowd. Agents should specialize too."

4. Attend local Small-Business Development Center (SBDC) seminars to learn how to start your own business, develop a business plan, and create a marketing strategy. (Go to http://sbdcnet.utsa.edu/sbdc.htm.) "Although the focus will be on typical retail and service businesses, real estate professionals should reword the examples to fit their own focus," Dacey says.

5. Envision your business. Read publications like *Adams Streetwise Small Business Start-Up: Your Comprehensive Guide to Starting and Managing a Business* by Bob Adams (Publisher: Adams Media Corporation, 1996, ISBN: 1558505814).

6. Track income and expenses. Use a program like Quick-Books basic accounting software and review monthly financial statements. (Go to http://quickbooks.intuit.com/.)

7. Name your business. Create a logo or identifying tag line, just as any new business would. In some states, due to licensing regulations, a business name may be for the agent's internal use only and not shared with the public. Check with your state's real estate commission for more information on this topic.

Existing agents who need a refresher course on business ownership should take the same steps outlined above. "No matter what stage of the game they're at, agents should revamp their internal image from 'real estate agent' to 'small-business owner,'" says Dacey. "The key is to embrace this new concept by following the steps recommended for all new business start-ups."

Cash Is King

When you start thinking like a small-business owner, finances will probably consume a good portion of your time not spent working with customers, selling homes. That's because for the small-business owner, cash flow is king. Without it, equipment can't be purchased, employees can't be paid, and business can't be conducted. The lifeblood of any company, cash flow includes currency, checks on hand, and bank deposits. Cash equivalents are short-term, temporary investments like treasury bills, certificates of deposit, or commercial paper that can be quickly and easily converted into cash.

Armed with those assets, a business can pay bills, repay loans, make investments, and provide goods and services to its customers. The cash also plays a critical role in generating even more cash when higher profits start to roll in. The fundamentals of cash flow seem simple enough, but the real question is: How does a small-business owner go about creating an accurate picture of the operation's cash flow?

First, create a cash flow statement that clearly documents the movement of cash in and out of your company in any given year. A cash flow statement reports a business's sources and uses of cash along with the beginning and ending values for cash and cash equivalents each year. It also includes the combined total change in cash and cash equivalents from all sources and uses of cash.

There are generally two methods for calculating cash flow from operating activities: indirect and direct.

Indirect Method

Popular because of its relative simplicity, the indirect method has you start with a figure for net income (from your income statement) and helps you adjust this accrual amount for any items that do not affect cash flows.

There are three basic types of adjustments:

1. Revenues and expenses that do not involve cash inflows or outflows (e.g., cost allocations such as depreciation and amortization)
2. Gains and losses on events reported in other sections of the statement of cash flows
3. Conversions of current operating assets and liabilities from the accrual to the cash basis

Direct Method

The direct method, although less popular, is favored by many financial managers because it reports the source of cash inflows and outflows directly, without the potentially confusing adjustments to net income.

Instead of starting with a reported net income, the direct method analyzes the various types of operating activities and calculates the total cash flow created by each one. Before beginning the direct method, all accrual accounts must first be converted to a cash figure.

Cash flow statements are broken down into three sections:

1. *Operating Activities:* The net amount of cash provided (or used) by operating activities is the key figure on a statement of cash flows. Operating activities (all transactions and events that normally enter into the determination of operating income) include cash receipts from selling goods or providing services, as well as income from items such as interest and dividends. Operating activities also include your cash payments for inventory, payroll, taxes, interest, utilities, and rent.

Note: Although cash inflows from interest or dividends could be considered investing or financing activities, the Financial Accounting Standards Board classifies them as operating activities (which means you probably should too).

2. *Investing Activities:* Investing activities include transactions and events involving the purchase and sale of securities (excluding cash equivalents), land, buildings, equipment, and other assets not generally held for resale. It also covers the making and collecting of loans. Investing activities are not classified as operating activities because they have an indirect relationship to the central, ongoing operation of your business (usually the sale of goods or services).

Cash receipts include:

❑ Sales of plant assets
❑ Sales of a business segment
❑ Sales of investments in equity securities of other entities or debt securities (other than cash equivalents)
❑ Collections of principal on loans made to other entities

Cash payments include:

❑ Purchases of plant assets
❑ Purchases of equity securities of other entities or debt securities (other than cash equivalents)
❑ Loans to other entities

3. *Financing Activities.* All financing activities deal with the flow of cash to or from the business owners (equity financing)

and creditors (debt financing). For example, cash proceeds from issuing capital stock or bonds would be classified under financing activities. Likewise, payments to repurchase stock (treasury stock) or to retire bonds and the payment of dividends are financing activities as well.

Cash receipts include:

❑ Issuances of own stock

❑ Borrowings (bonds, notes, mortgages, etc.)

Cash payments include:

❑ Dividends to stockholders

❑ Repayment of principal amounts borrowed

❑ Repurchases of business's own stock (treasury stock)

Once you've created a cash flow statement for your company, you'll gain a much better understanding of your company's financial position and be able to make more informed decisions regarding its future. A cash flow statement is important to your business because it can be used to assess the timing, amount, and predictability of future cash flows. It can be the basis for budgeting—a very important issue in the real estate industry, where commission checks can be spaced out by wide gaps without any cash flow. A cash flow statement can answer questions like, "Where did the money come from?" or "Where did it go?"

To Incorporate or Not?

One way to really start feeling like a small-business owner is by incorporating your business, although not all new agents will want to take this step fresh out of real estate school. Once the commissions start rolling in, you may want to join the ranks of business owners who have shed their sole proprietorships in favor of corporations. Nationally, about 5 million U.S. corporations bring in $17 trillion in sales each year, according to research company BizStats.com.

Gene Fairbrother, lead small-business consultant for the National Association for the Self-Employed (NASE) in Dallas, Texas, says issues surrounding incorporation are a hot topic for his group's 250,000 members. "It's a major issue and the number one or number two question that our Shop Talk consultants work through with small-business owners," says Fairbrother. "I'd venture to say incorporating is the most predominant issue for micro and small businesses right now."

Business owners are generally most concerned with which legal entity to select, afraid that the incorrect choice may hurt their companies. Basic choices include the partnership, the C corporation (a traditional corporation), and the subchapter S corporation. Chartered by the state in which it is headquartered, the corporation is considered by law to be a unique entity, separate and apart from those who own it, according to the U.S. Small Business Administration.

A corporation can be taxed and sued, and can enter into contractual agreements. The owners of a corporation are its shareholders, who elect a board of directors to oversee the major policies and decisions. The corporation has a life of its own and does not dissolve when ownership changes. The S corporation is a tax election that enables shareholders to treat the earnings and profits as distributions and have them pass through directly to their personal tax returns. The shareholders (if working for the company, and if there is a profit) must pay themselves and must meet standards of "reasonable compensation."

A relatively new option is the limited liability company (LLC), defined as a "hybrid business structure that is now permissible in most states." The LLC is designed to provide the limited liability features of a corporation and the tax efficiencies and operational flexibility of a partnership, though formation is more complex and formal than that of a general partnership.

To get more information about business incorporation, surf over to the U.S. Small Business Administration (SBA) Web site at (www.sba.gov) or visit your local bookstore or library to get more information about small-business incorporation. Do this before making any selections or investing any money in the process. Steer clear of companies making claims like "Incorporate in Delaware or Nevada for $200," as such outfits aren't credible and can lead to major headaches for the business owner.

"Do your homework," says Fairbrother. "Get some professional guidance, research the options, and then select the entity that fits well with your own business goals and aspirations."

And remember that incorporating is more than just filing paperwork. Agents should always seek help from a small-business CPA or attorney, who will probably charge about $600 to $1,000 for professional assistance provided throughout the process. Thoroughly research the different entities, because in some cases an LLC may be a better choice than a corporation.

Also be sure to check with your state real estate licensing agency to see if it allows individual agents to incorporate. In Florida, for example, brokers can incorporate with little restriction but agents can use only the name appearing on their license with the designation P.A. after it. The P.A. stands for Professional Association. This notifies the public that an owner who is licensed by the state of Florida is the primary purveyor of services sold. Typically this designation is seen after a medical group's name or CPA practice.

Here's a quick look at the pros and cons of incorporating your real estate business:

❑ Benefits:

    ○ Opportunity to select subchapter S corporate tax treatment, which can lower an agent's cost of Social Security and Medicare tax (15 percent savings on a portion of profits).

    ○ Liability protection from acts of competently managed employees.

    ○ Easier to qualify for corporate discounts with companies like Barnes & Noble or Borders.

    ○ Easier to qualify for contractor credit cards offered by building supply companies like Home Depot and Lowe's.

    ○ Easier to qualify for reward programs offered by office supply stores like Office Max or Staples.

    ○ Helps solidify the agent's self image as a small business.

    ○ Not restricted on losses to two years out of five like sole proprietorships are generally held to by the IRS.

❑ Downfalls:

    ○ Additional annual cost of having a corporate tax return prepared (usually $395 to $895).

    ○ Annual cost of the state corporate renewal fee. (Varies state to state. In Florida it is currently $150.)

    ○ May be subject to additional local or state occupational license fees or business assessments.

    ○ The agent must become an employee of the corporation. Payroll requires additional paperwork and compliance requirements.

    ○ Additional cost of consulting a CPA or knowledgeable adviser to ensure the agent is aware of new responsibilities or compliance issues.

Source: Judith E. Dacey, CPA

See Table 8-1 for a comparison of business entities.

Table 8-1. Comparison of business entities.

Issues	Sole Prop	Partnership	LLC	C Corp	S Corp
Limited liability	No	No for general partner	Yes	Yes	Yes
Continuity of existence	No	Possible by agreement	Possible by agreement	Yes	Yes
Transferability of interest	No	Possible by agreement	Possible by agreement	Yes	Yes
Administrative, legal & accounting costs	Least	More	Most	Most	Most
Taxation of income	Directly to owner. Subject to Social Security & Medicare taxes.	Directly to each partner. Subject to Social Security & Medicare taxes.	If single member, like sole prop. If 2+ owners, like a partnership.	Taxed on corp. level & taxed again on individual level when dividends are distributed.	Taxed directly to shareholders. Not subject to Social Security.
Deductibility of losses (subject to at-risk rules)	Yes	Yes, if active partner	N/A	Only by corporation	By shareholders
Allocation of taxable income & losses to multiple owners	N/A	Can be allocated in any manner, as agreed	N/A	Must be allocated by % of stock owned	Must be allocated by % of stock owned

©2004 Judith E. Dacey, CPA

Good Reasons

For real estate agents, incorporating can be particularly com-pelling, not so much for tax reasons but for the protection that such entities provide to their shareholders. Working in an in-creasingly litigious society, where real estate agents have be-come the target of lawsuits ranging from poor property disclosures to toxic-mold cases, some consider it wise to incor-porate as a way to protect your assets from lawsuits.

William Bronchick is an author and attorney who regularly presents workshops and do-it-yourself seminars at real estate and landlord associations around the country. As president and cofounder of the Colorado Association of Real Estate Investors, Bronchick gives these nine reasons to incorporate a real estate business:

1. *Protection from Personal Liability:* If you do business in your own name, you are risking everything you have. A corporation will separate your business from your personal assets. If one of your agents commits wrongdoing, your corporation will be held liable, but not you personally.

2. *Less Risk of Audit:* If you are a broker, property manager, or anyone else who reports income on a Schedule C, you are a high risk for an IRS audit. The IRS audits Schedule C businesses much more often than small corporations. Simply by incorporating, you may reduce your risk of an audit by as much as 300 percent.

3. *Liquidity:* Everyone knows of real estate companies that have their owners' names all over them. In fact, without that person, the business has no name. The point is, you can't sell a business if it relies primarily on you. You need to set up an entity that stands apart from you that can be sold as an ongoing business.

4. *Fringe Benefits:* Items like health insurance, medical costs, and life insurance are not fully deductible as an individual business owner. However, if you set up a C corporation, you can deduct 100 percent of your medical insurance and medical expenses, and up to $50,000 of term life insurance. Keep in mind that these benefits must be offered to all of your full-time employees as well.

5. *Tax Savings:* A corporation can be an excellent device for turning nondeductible expenses into deductible expenses. For

example, the old "home office" is a trap for small-business people who try to claim the expense on their personal tax return. However, if your corporation leased the same space from your home, you reduce the risk of being audited for the same deduction.

6. *Income Splitting:* If you operate as a sole proprietor, you are taxed on all profits you make, even if you reinvest the money into the business. A C corporation is a separate taxpayer from you. The corporation pays its own tax, but usually at a lower rate than you pay (C corporation tax is only 15 percent up to $50,000). If you take a small salary and leave the rest of the profit in your corporation, you can effectively reduce your overall income tax.

7. *Prestige:* In the business world, a corporate entity just looks better. People will think you are savvier if you are "North American Realty, Inc." rather than "John Smith Realty."

8. *Privacy:* A corporation gives you privacy from prying eyes. It also gives you a buffer zone from your tenants. You don't want your customers to know you are the owner. You are at a distinct negotiating disadvantage when you are the "greedy landlord." Instead, you should represent that you are an employee of the management corporation. That way, you are just the "go between."

9. *Portability:* Real estate cannot get up and walk away. If a corporation owns your real estate, it can be moved easily, since the corporate stock can be transferred. If your real estate is owned in a corporation or other entity that has transferable ownership, the ownership goes where you go. This is important in estate planning. If you own real estate in more than one state, your heirs must go through probate proceedings in each state. By converting the real estate into personal property (stock certificates), there will be a need for probate only in the state in which you die.

At Coldwell Banker Apex, Realtors in Dallas, Lori Arnold says her company advises all of its agents to consider incorporating. She generally directs the agent to a qualified accountant who can also help that person sock away a certain amount of each commission check for quarterly estimated tax payments and other expenses. "We absolutely advocate incorporating, when the situation warrants it," says Arnold.

Reaping Rewards

When you start operating like a business owner—and not just an individual real estate agent who has hung her license with a local brokerage company—you'll open yourself up to a number of benefits generally reserved only for legitimate businesses. They include, but are not limited to:

❏ Creating long-term, professional relationships with banks, accountants, financial planners, and others who can help you start and grow your entity

❏ Establishing strong bonds with business groups, trade associations, and organizations, which in turn translate into more customers and referrals

❏ Access to bank lines of credit, loans, and U.S. Small Business Administration–guaranteed loans

❏ Recognition in the community, and opportunities to raise your company's profile by tapping sponsorship opportunities that range from Little League teams to cultural events, and everything in between

Because it can take time to start earning revenue as a real estate agent, one particularly good resource for agents just starting up or seeking growth funding is the SBA (www.sba

.gov). Whether you're in need of start-up capital or an infusion of cash to grow your existing company, this government entity is a logical first step on your road to getting financed. The organization doesn't make loans itself, but specializes in a host of loan-guaranty programs that banks rely on when lending money to small companies.

For entrepreneurs interested in an SBA loan, the most popular choice is the group's 7(a) Loan Guaranty program. Through it, private lenders will make loans to your business that the SBA will guarantee up to 85 percent (on loans up to $150,000) or 75 percent (on those more than $150,000) of, up to a maximum guarantee of $1 million. To apply for this loan you must obtain an application from a local SBA lender in your area.

Before you sit down with your banker, you'll need to get a handle on how much money you need, what it will be used for, and how it will be repaid. Existing businesses should also provide a history of the company and how it has performed since inception, as well as financial records such as a profit and loss statement for the last three years.

If your loan is approved, the bank funds it and the SBA guarantees a certain percentage based on the loan amount. If approved, the loans can be for working capital to buy inventory, furniture and fixtures, machinery and equipment, land for construction, building construction, leasehold improvements, and real property.

From the small businesses it guarantees, the lender is looking for repayment ability from the cash flow of the business, good character, management capability, collateral, and owner's equity contribution. All owners of 20 percent or more are required to personally guarantee SBA loans; the average 7(a) loan size was $236,000 in 2002.

The SBA loan guaranties can be especially helpful for small businesses that can't come up with the collateral requirement that commercial lenders typically require. Most small businesses don't have a lot of collateral because they don't own their buildings, tend to be small in size, and have limited tangible assets that can be posted for collateral. This is an issue for a commercial lender working one-on-one with a small business, but lenders see things differently when the SBA guarantees the loan.

If your financial requirements are less than $150,000, there are other SBA-backed loans that require very little documentation. The SBA LowDoc (low documentation) program, for example, was created for fast processing (the SBA says approval time is thirty-six hours or less) and requires just a one-page application. Approval is based mainly on strength of character and the applicant's credit. The same process applies as the 7(a) loan in that selected lenders make the actual loans to start-ups and small companies with fewer than 100 employees.

If $35,000 or less will work for your company, then a good, low-hassle option is the SBA MicroLoan program, where the average loan size is $10,500. Through the program, the SBA makes funds available to nonprofit, community-based lenders (known as *intermediaries*), which, in turn, make loans to eligible borrowers. Again, you'll need to submit an application to a local lender that works with the SBA for a credit decision.

One of the first things any lender will consider during the loan process is credit history. Most lenders also use the following "five Cs of credit analysis," to determine your loan eligibility:

1. *Capacity* to repay is the most critical of the five factors. The prospective lender will want to know exactly how you intend to repay the loan and will consider the cash flow from the business, the timing of the repayment, and the probability of successful repayment of the loan.

2. *Capital* is the money you personally have invested in the business and is an indication of how much you have at risk should the business fail.

3. *Collateral* is an additional form of security you can provide the lender. Giving a lender collateral means that you pledge an asset you own, such as your home, to the lender with the agreement that it will be the repayment source in case you can't repay the loan.

4. *Conditions* focus on the intended purpose of the loan. Will the money be used for working capital, additional equipment, or inventory?

5. *Character* is the general impression you make on the potential lender or investor. The lender will form a subjective opinion about whether you are sufficiently trustworthy to repay the loan or generate a return on funds invested in your company.

On the Web

Today's agents have a valuable tool, literally at their fingertips, that many before them didn't have: the Web. Unfortunately, too many of them approach the medium with an unprofessional stance, again forgetting they're not employees of a company, but owners of their own companies. There are many resources available on the market that cover the basics of Web site design and marketing, but here's a good starting point for any agent looking to "up" his profile on the Web.

Lured by the excitement of the World Wide Web, many companies rush to set up shop online without proper planning or research. Armed with good intentions and a desire to get a piece of the Internet pie, these entrepreneurs are unaware that:

❑ A shoddy Web site portrays a negative company image.

❑ Rushing into it can be costly, in terms of both time and money.

❑ A poorly designed Web site can actually drive customers away—precisely what they *didn't* want their Web site to do!

What entrepreneurs should know is that WWW doesn't stand for "Wild, Wild West" anymore, and that many small-business owners have tried and succeeded (and, tried and failed), on the Web, leaving behind valuable, well-documented lessons for you to follow. From well-known sites like Amazon .com, Dell.com, and Realtor.com, to those created by smaller companies, they're all right at your fingertips.

The news gets even better: If you're developing a Web site for your small business, then you're already ahead of the game. According to a recent Verizon SuperPages.com survey, just 37 percent of small businesses even have a Web site. Of those that do, few can say their sites actually boost company sales. Instead, most serve as glorified marketing tools that help keep up with competitors and improve customer services.

With the help of a good Web designer and some in-depth research on your competitors' sites (and the industry's most successful sites), your own site won't fall into that trap. Remember these key issues when operating on the Web:

❑ *Remember—first impressions count:* Think about the product and/or service you're selling, and paint a picture of your target customer. Then design your Web site around what is important to that group.

❑ *Solve their problems:* Put yourself in your customers' shoes: do you only want to be shown a bunch of products, or would you rather be told how that product could solve one of your problems? Most people are moved by the latter, so avoid overwhelming visitors with a bunch of products on the first page. Instead, sell them a solution.

❑ *Reward loyal customers:* Don't let your best customers—those who buy time and time again—feel undervalued. Entice the exceptional customers, not just the average ones, by polling them about what they would like to see on your site.

❑ *Serve the customer:* Invest as much as possible in customer service. If that means hiring more customer service reps or buying a better phone system to facilitate your customer calls, do it.

❑ *Make it hard to leave:* That doesn't mean a lengthy checkout process, of course, just an attractive, helpful site that includes the best product, service, and price and a fulfillment system that makes defecting to another site unthinkable.

Walk the Walk

In this chapter we covered several business-related issues that real estate agents need to be aware of and stressed the need for a business ownership mindset when working in the business. By thinking and operating like a business owner, you'll be more apt to break out from under your broker's wing and start promoting yourself and your services by taking active roles in Realtor and related organizations, sponsoring events, and marketing yourself with a vengeance. Here are some other steps you can take to get yourself thinking like a business owner:

❑ Cut yourself a paycheck every week, two weeks, or month, instead of just dropping your commission checks into your personal bank account.

❏ Get on a regular schedule of depositing estimated quarterly taxes.

❏ Create an image for your business that includes your photo, logo, and a short tagline (such as "Your leader for exceptional real estate service") to use on all correspondence, advertisements, and other materials.

❏ Investigate the possibility of incorporating, and research the various entities that are available to you as a real estate agent in your state.

❏ Adopt the philosophy that it takes money to make money, and don't be afraid to make affordable investments in technology, tools, office supplies, or other materials that will help you reach new customers and/or retain the ones you already have.

❏ At the same time, keep tabs on your business expenses and spend only what your business can cover without putting yourself in the red.

❏ Operate with the highest of ethical and legal standards at all times.

If you've spent a lot of time working in a salaried or hourly position, handling these and other business-related issues will be quite a change for you. Take heed because you're certainly not alone. Every year thousands of people make the pilgrimage from Corporate America to the real estate industry, seeking out new opportunities, more flexible work schedules, and a more gratifying career.

It's not always easy for them. One agent tells the story of how he struggled to learn how to sell himself, instead of selling a product, brand, or company. Coming from a thirty-nine-year career in Corporate America, where he worked in sales for a forest products manufacturer, the agent spent his first few months in real estate learning how to market himself as an individual agent.

"In Corporate America I was well grounded. I knew exactly who I was and where I fit into the business and the industry," says the agent, who within four months had already sold one home and listed another.

"Taking the path of an independent agent has been a whole different world for me," says the agent, who has since come to realize that although real estate requires a degree of teamwork, success really depends on how well agents can operate as business owners and truly differentiate themselves in a competitive marketplace.

As this agent learned, the key is to take it step by step, knowing that as each day passes it will become easier and easier to adopt the mindset of a business owner, rather than an employee. If you need more help getting your business on track, try one or more of these business resources:

❑ *Accounting and Financial Professionals:* A quick review of your financial statements by a trained eye can help detect slow collections, poor financial management, overextended accounts payables, or other warning signs early. Financial advisers can provide similar services. Accountants can be a big asset when it comes to issues like taxes and incorporating. Get referrals through the National Association of Personal Financial Advisers (www.napfa.org) and the AICPA (www.aicpa.org).

❑ *Financial Institutions:* Visit your bank for assistance with a line of credit, accounts receivable loan, or other vehicle to ease the cash crunch. Banks also provide ancillary services for their small-business customers: Wells Fargo (www.wellsfargo .com/biz), for example, offers an assistance program especially for African American small-business owners.

❏ *Business Groups:* Groups like the SBA, SCORE, and groups like the National Minority Supplier Development Council, Inc. offer programs and guidance for small-business owners with financial questions. Visit www.sba.gov, www.score.org, and www.nmsdcus.org for more information.

CHAPTER NINE

Long-Term Planning

"IT'S NOT THE PLAN THAT IS IMPORTANT,

IT'S THE PLANNING."

—DR. GRAEME EDWARDS

In their quest to handle the day-to-day real estate tasks, keep those commission checks coming in, and manage a plethora of new and existing clients, real estate agents tend to woefully neglect themselves. Because no employer is socking away money for them in a retirement account, providing health insurance benefits, or giving them stock options, agents who overlook this aspect of their business can find themselves in trouble down the road.

To determine if you're one of these agents, answer yes or no to the following six questions and check your score at the end of the quiz.

1. Do I have a mechanism in place for investing in my future?
2. Do I have health insurance coverage for myself and my family (if applicable)?
3. Do I have life insurance?
4. Do I have a means of providing long-term care for elderly family members, if necessary?
5. If I have children, have I established a means of investing for their college education?
6. Have I sat down with a financial planner within the last five years to discuss my nest egg and other relevant financial topics?

Scoring:

5–6 yes answers: You're well on your way to having a solid plan in place for your future.

3–4 yes answers: You're getting there, but you'll definitely want to look at some of the "no" areas to see where you can beef up your long-term planning.

1–2 yes answers: Time to take a step back from your day-to-day workload and do some long-term financial planning for yourself and your family.

If your score wasn't up to par, you're not alone. Most financial professionals know that inadequate long-term planning is endemic among small-business owners, including real estate agents. "The biggest challenge for agents is making time for themselves to create—and then commit to—a business, financial, and life plan," says Rich Arzaga, wealth planner with AIG Advisor Group in Walnut Creek, California, "and to understand how their current work ties into their goals."

That's because successful real estate agents tend to have a consistent internal wiring that allows them to prosper, regardless of market conditions or the economy. They react quickly, focus on client needs, and even place those clients' needs ahead of their own. Unfortunately, these business strengths can also be weaknesses.

"Real estate agents tend to subordinate their own business-, financial-, and life-planning matters to the practice of real estate," says Arzaga, a former real estate professional who often works with agents and brokers, helping them create long-term plans for financial success. In doing so, he's noticed that real estate agents postpone personal financial planning meetings at least five times more often than non–real estate clients—mainly because they're spending time on listing presentations, open houses, and mailings.

On the bright side, Arzaga says real estate agents have access to significant benefits that other small-business owners may not have at their fingertips, including:

- ❏ The ability to build a long-term referral business to ensure long-term value for their practice
- ❏ The ability to distinguish themselves strategically by creating a network of resources for their clients
- ❏ The ability to be well versed in investment real estate
  and serve a niche that is sorely lacking
- ❏ The ability to invest in real estate and be advantaged by
  cost savings, rebates, and referral fees
- ❏ The ability to be extremely aggressive in their retirement
  planning
- ❏ The ability to scale their business up (or down) while
  keeping a tight lid on expenses
- ❏ The ability to move their business fairly easily if it suits
  them

The irony is that many successful agents who have been
in the business a reasonable amount of time desperately look
forward to cutting back their work, or getting out of the business entirely. Yet, very few know what that looks like financially. "Very few people (and even fewer agents) understand
the financial capital needed to maintain their existing standard
of living during financial independence (retirement)," Arzaga
states. "And even fewer understand the impact of taxes, inflation, Social Security, or working part-time."

The statistics prove it: According to AARP, 80 percent of
people age 65 or older are unable to maintain a comfortable
standard of living for themselves. Most find themselves looking
for more affordable places to live, dramatically cutting expenses (very tough to do at that stage in someone's life), or
working part- to full-time to meet their needs.

To avoid falling into that trap, real estate agents need to
begin their long-term planning well before they're no longer

willing—or able—to work. The longer the time horizon to financial independence, the more options and alternatives the agent has. "I've seen too many times that an agent and his/her spouse, ages 50 or older, are on track to outlive their money because they failed to plan," says Arzaga. "There is no better hedge to successful planning than planning as far in advance of retirement as possible."

Early Steps

To create an effective long-term plan for personal and financial success in real estate, you'll want to revisit some of the basic business planning concepts covered in chapters 1 through 8 of this book. Here's a synopsis of the key steps you should be taking:

- ❑ Make sure you go into the business with your eyes open, and with the support of your significant other.
- ❑ Create a business and marketing plan that is attainable and that creates accountability.
- ❑ Work with a professional to get a snapshot of your financial condition (including key components like assets, cash flow, and estate planning).
- ❑ Make sure all assets are optimized based on your own unique risk tolerance (defined as the degree of negative change that an investor can handle in the value of his portfolio).
- ❑ Control business and household expenses by tracking the last twelve months' expenses and by setting a budget going forward.

❏ Make sure your current financial condition, personal financial goals, and business planning objectives are aligned.

❏ Provide for an appropriate level of reserves to launch your business and to sustain some of the market swings and seasonality.

❏ Measure your success, and make adjustments when appropriate.

Once an agent has experienced success in the industry—and starts to bring in a reasonable level of discretionary income—exploring appropriate retirement plans and other strategies to defer or reduce taxes becomes critical. And although many experienced agents feel that the highest amount they can tuck away in a tax-deferred retirement account is $40,000 to $60,000 (annually), new rules regarding retirement accounts actually allow plan owners to defer as much as $175,000 or more each year, based on income.

With a retirement plan, you can not only sock away pretax dollars, you can also reduce tax liabilities by setting up and funding such accounts. They've come a long way in the last few years. If you aren't taking advantage of this self-employment benefit, you're not alone. According to the Internal Revenue Service, just 5 percent of small-business owners and employees are covered by retirement plans.

Here's a look at the three popular retirement options for agents:

SIMPLE IRA

❏ Key advantage: Salary-reduction plan with little administrative paperwork.

❏ Eligibility: Any business with 100 or fewer employees that does not currently maintain any other retirement plan.

❏ Your responsibilities: Set up by completing IRS Form 5304-SIMPLE or 5305-SIMPLE. No employer tax filing required. The bank or financial institution handles the bulk of the paperwork.

❏ Maximum annual contribution per participant: Employee—$9,000 for 2004 (or $10,500 for those aged 50 or older). Employer—Either match employee contributions dollar for dollar up to 3 percent of compensation or contribute 2 percent of each eligible employee's compensation.

❏ Minimum employee coverage: Must be offered to all employees who have earned at least $5,000 in the previous two years.

SEP-IRA

❏ Key advantage: Easy to set up and maintain.

❏ Eligibility: Any business with one or more employees.

❏ Your responsibilities: Set up a plan by completing IRS Form 5305-SEP. No employer tax filing required.

❏ Maximum annual contribution per participant: For 2004, the lesser amount of 25 percent of compensation or $41,000.

❏ Minimum employee coverage: Must be offered to all employees who are at least 21 years of age, have been employed by the business for three of the last five years, and have earned at least $450 in a year.

401(k)

❏ Key advantage: Permits employee to contribute more than in other options.

❏ Eligibility: Any business with one or more employee.

❏ Your responsibilities: Consult with a financial institution or employee benefit provider, as there is no model form used to establish a plan. The plan requires an annual filing of IRS Form 5500 and special testing to ensure that it does not discriminate in favor of highly compensated employees.

❏ Maximum annual contribution per participant: Employee—$13,000 for 2004. Employer/Employee combined—Up to a maximum of 25 percent of compensation or $40,000. Note that 2004 total additions cannot exceed the lesser of $41,000 or 100 percent of compensation. If you are age 50 or older, they cannot exceed the lesser of $44,000 or 100 percent of compensation.

❏ Minimum employee coverage: Must be offered to all employees at least 21 years of age who worked at least 1,000 hours during the previous year.

Before selecting a retirement plan, you'll want to discuss your strategy with a financial adviser or accountant who can fill you in on any new details, requirements, or drawbacks to certain plans.

Strategizing for Success

While you're discussing a retirement planning strategy, you'll also want to tap the expert's knowledge on the following issues:

❏ Creating a comprehensive plan that aligns your business and financial matters with your own personal goals.

❏ Planning seriously for events that would negatively impact planning, like long-term care, disability, and certainly death. (How will the ones left behind be provided for?)

❑ Taking the time to focus on the endgame by asking yourself:

   ○ What will happen when I leave the business?

   ○ What type of business succession and continuity planning should I have in place to optimize the future value of the practice I've built?

   ○ What type of legacy in the business do I want to leave, and how will I accomplish this?

❑ Thinking further into the future, by asking yourself:

   ○ How do I want to have my estate distributed when I pass?

   ○ Whom will I enrich, and how will I go about doing this?

   ○ Is my estate plan appropriate, and does it account for the future value of my assets?

   ○ Have I created a plan that will pass almost everything to my beneficiaries and minimizes estate taxes and probate costs?

   ○ Have these documents been reviewed recently?

   ○ Is the titling of my assets appropriate for my estate plan?

Once you've tackled these big-picture items, you'll want to drill down on a few key financial planning points. If you choose to work with a financial planner, this person will probably go over each of these components. If you're doing it on your own, here's a look at the various aspects of your personal and business life that should be addressed in order to create a complete plan:

❑ Current situation, risk tolerance, time horizon, and personal and financial goals

❏ Cash flow

❏ Retirement planning

❏ Retirement distribution

❏ Investment planning

❏ Tax strategies

❏ Estate planning (or for high-net-worth individuals, wealth preservation)

❏ Education planning

❏ Special needs (disabilities, senior dependents)

❏ Risk management (death, disability, long-term care)

❏ Survivorship

❏ Accumulation needs (weddings, vacation home, boat)

❏ Educational needs

❏ Business succession and continuity

❏ Immediate cash needs (reserves)

Expect to spend about $2,500 (give or take a few dollars, depending on your needs and your geographic location) for a financial planner's assistance with this process. Also expect to meet with the professional about five or six times (for a total of eight to ten hours over the course of a month or two) to work out the details and get the plan into shape. Here's a look at how Arzaga divides up that time when working with clients:

❏ First meeting: Preliminary data gathering—mostly questions for the agent about family, goals, anxieties, current assets and cash flow, and current estate plan.

❏ Second meeting: If there appears to be both a need and a match, then he goes into comprehensive data gathering (qualitative and quantitative) of statistics, documents, and dreams.

❏ Third meeting: Preliminary plan design for all relevant areas of planning, based on the client's needs. For example, a couple with no kids would not likely need education planning.

❏ Fourth meeting: Testing suitable concepts and strategies that meet the agent's objectives.

❏ Fifth meeting: Final plan presentation.

❏ Sixth meeting: Implementation of the plan, then a periodic, scheduled review of the plan (generally on a semiannual basis, with quarterly reports provided to the agent).

Other Considerations

Regardless of what path you take in creating a long-term plan for your business and life, there are a few key elements that you won't want to neglect. In addition to those already discussed, here are a few other building blocks that you'll want to take into consideration when working on your own plan:

❏ *Health Insurance:* These days, health insurance is a big concern for everyone—particularly for small-business owners. No one seems to have a handle on this, except to line up with some type of employer that offers lifetime benefits, or project higher-than-average cost increases to pay the premiums. Unless they're fortunate enough to have a spouse with a full-time job and benefits, most real estate agents grapple with the issue of health insurance coverage at some point during their career. Joining them in the struggle are a large number of self-employed professionals who—particularly in recent years—have found themselves shut out of the affordable health insurance market.

In a December 2003 study, the Kaiser Family Foundation reported that over 60 percent of the nation's uninsured workers are either employed by small companies or self-employed.

Workers employed in companies with fewer than 100 employees run the highest risk of being uninsured, according to Kaiser, which reports that 27 percent of those workers are now uninsured. Exacerbating the problem of access are skyrocketing rates. Kaiser reports that private health insurance premiums rose 13.9 percent in 2003 over 2002, representing the third consecutive year of double-digit increases and the largest jump since 1990.

See the sidebar "Health Insurance for Realtors" for a discussion of the NAR's response to this issue.

❏ *Other Types of Insurance:* Having suitable amounts for property and casualty insurance is equally as important, especially for real estate agents. Umbrella insurance offers the highest ratio of benefit to cost, and is a good way to protect an estate. Life insurance is another important planning tool and generally comprises three phases: insurance to provide for the ongoing existence and support of the family (lower- and middle-class), self-insurance (upper-class), and insurance as an estate-planning strategy (affluent).

❏ *College Educations:* As a parent, the world is your oyster right now when it comes to college savings. Families can plan to cover all, most, or some of their children's anticipated costs, and grandparents and other family members can be rallied to do the same. There are also grants, scholarships, state prepaid, and 529 plans, among others. "There are some types of resources for most people for most circumstances," says Arzaga, who adds that planning is the key to success in this area. Some of the trickier aspects of college planning include what school (or more like what tuition) to target, in state or out, room and board or stay at home, and the future cost of college. There are so many variables that it might make sense to have a progressive plan in place, with the 529 plan being one of the best choices. You can learn more about college savings options on-line at: www.savingforcollege.com.

❑ *Real Estate Investments:* With the stock market in the dol-drums over the last few years, real estate has become a very hot area for agents and other investors. For those who aren't ready to go out and buy property, Real Estate Investment Trusts (REITS, which are companies that invest in real estate or real estate–related assets) are a good way to hold this asset for the more conservative and smaller investor.

❑ *Long-Term Care (LTC) for Elderly Parents:* With the na-tion's elderly population on the rise, LTC has become a hot issue for everyone, yet most people have no plan in place to address the issues of a protracted illness. If in need of a rehabil-itative, therapeutic, diagnostic, maintenance, or personal-care service in a setting other than an acute-care unit of a hospital (such as a nursing home or your own residence), these costs would have to be provided by your personal assets. According to Arzaga, the likelihood of needing long-term care and the fi-nancial consequences of it are surprisingly high, based on these facts:

  ○ Roughly, half of all persons over 65 will spend some time in a nursing home.
  ○ The average stay is approximately 2½ years.
  ○ Average costs exceed $52,000 annually.
  ○ Medicare covers only about 2 percent of these costs.

For these and other reasons, you'll definitely want to incor-porate LTC into any long-term planning that you do as an agent, or risk having to deal with larger consequences down the road.

The Long-Term View

There's no time like the present to take a long-term view of your real estate career and create a plan for developing your business and providing a stable future for yourself and your family. Getting there requires a well-rounded view of your own finances and your financial goals, and a measurement of what kind of risk you're willing to take to get there. Here are some examples for various stages of the business:

❑ *New Real Estate Agent:* Fresh out of real estate school, a new agent lacks the financial means and wherewithal to create a complete financial plan, but that doesn't mean she can't:
   ○ Shop around for a good health insurance plan for herself.
   ○ Shell out a small fee to start a SEP-IRA plan for her future.
   ○ Purchase a term life insurance policy.

❑ *Agent with Two Years of Experience:* An agent with two years under his belt and a child who is six years away from college will want to take all of the steps mentioned above, plus:
   ○ Sit down with a financial planner to incorporate more elements into a long-term plan for personal financial success.
   ○ Start a 529 or other college savings plan.
   ○ Consider a retirement plan that allows for larger contributions (such as a 401(k) plan).
   ○ Think about investing in real estate as part of his overall investment portfolio.
   ○ Factor in other issues like long-term care and investment accounts (such as mutual funds or individual stocks).

❑ *Agent with Ten Years of Experience:* Depending on the agent's financial situation, and just how much planning she's done along the way, this agent will want to take all of the steps outlined above, plus:

HEALTH INSURANCE FOR REALTORS

When this book went to press, the National Association of Realtors was offering its members a new weapon for their health insurance arsenal. The group has joined forces with Marsh Affinity Group Services to provide insurance benefits to the country's Realtors.

Through NAR's Realtor VIP Alliance Program, members can access top industry insurance carriers that offer health, life, dental, and disability insurance. NAR members as well as national, state, and local staff and their immediate families are eligible. Part of the Marsh & McLennan family of companies, Marsh currently serves the health and welfare needs of more than 1,000 affinity organizations and is the largest third-party administrator of association insurance programs in the world.

Marsh offers underwritten health coverage for individuals and small groups of two to 50 with a variety of options, including preferred provider organizations (PPOs), health maintenance organizations (HMOs), point of service (POS), indemnity, and medical savings accounts (MSAs). Short-term and catastrophic options are also available, as well as a cancer care protection option.

Life coverage features include a choice of benefits, which do not reduce due to age, economical group rates, and choice of beneficiary. The dental coverage plan covers diagnostic treatments, preventive care, basic care (extractions, crowns, fillings), and major care (endodontics, periodontics, oral surgery, repairs to crowns, dentures, and bridges). The plan pays for dental expenses according to a schedule of benefits, which can be paid directly to the insured or can be assigned directly to a dentist.

Learn more about NAR's health insurance coverage online at www.seaburychicago.com/pp-nar/use home.htm.

INVESTING IN REAL ESTATE

Armed with an inherent and learned knowledge of real estate and how the buying and selling process works, real estate brokers and agents can make very good candidates for commercial and residential real estate investment. Making the option particularly attractive are the nation's rising property values, which have helped investors post significant gains on their real estate portfolios in a short period of time. Disenchanted with the stock market slump and enticed by low mortgage interest rates, many investors have turned to real estate as a safe haven for their hard-earned dollars.

Take one broker, who started working for Century 21 in 1989 and immediately began adding properties to his own portfolio. Back then, getting financed was a challenge, so the agent went after anything with owner financing that he could get his hands on, namely condominiums and single-family homes. "I bought the stuff that wasn't selling," says the agent, who today buys tracts of land for residential development.

He works together with partners who put up the cash for the purchases, then handles the entire process from start to finish. "It works out tremendously well," says the agent. Whether he's buying a one-bedroom condo or a forty-acre tract of land, the key to success is to lay out a plan before buying. He also takes into consideration the different demands for each type of property. For vacant land, grass must be cut and taxes paid long before any development is complete. When buying a duplex, however, the agent knows he'll have two rental incomes coming in, right out of the block.

Like any good agent would, this investor also relies on his own industry experience and sheer instinct to help during the decision-making process. "Very often," he adds, "I can just look at a piece of property and the ideas start popping into my head."

○ Consider any key tax strategies that will allow her to keep more income.

○ Meet annually with her financial planner to make adjustments to the long-term plan.

○ Regularly review all insurance policies to make sure they're current and in line with her life goals and financial position.

When planning for the long-term, there are a few important matters to keep in mind, whether you're a brand new agent or one who has been in the industry for ten years.

❏ Keep an eye on taxes, as there are very good strategies for reducing taxes that business owners can legitimately use.

❏ Look to increase contributions not only to add to retirement plans, but also to fund other parts of your plan (such as insurance and education).

❏ Always keep your personal goals in mind, and tie your financial decisions in with your overall financial plan.

❏ Refresh your plan every three to four years, or upon the occurrence of a major event.

❏ As your business grows and prospers, make sure that your current plan accounts for the additional cash flow and minimizes taxes.

As you work your way through the various components involved with long-term planning for success, remember that a one-size-fits-all approach probably won't work. By first examining your own business aspirations, life goals, and responsibilities, then leveraging them with a customized, comprehensive plan, your chances of achieving those goals will increase exponentially.

"During my last fifty first-time meetings with prospective clients, the outcome was different for each," Arzaga comments. "There are some common problem areas (estate planning, cash flow, expenses, retirement planning, retirement distribution, coordination of investments, and suitability of investments), but because of each agent's unique risk tolerance, time horizon, current situation, and goals, the advice and plans are always very different."

To those agents who have yet to consider the bigger picture, Arzaga says, "start planning now." The longer you wait, the fewer options that may be available, based on tax law changes, age limitations, and other issues beyond your control. The sooner you start, the more certainty and control you will have of the outcome.

"Financial planning gives people a great sense of comfort and freedom. Even for those whose trajectory appears that they may outlive their money, it gives them a sense of awareness, the ability to make adjustments, and a little more control," Arzaga adds. "Real estate agents thrive on control, and unbeknownst to most, a financial and/or business plan is a roadmap to ultimate control: financial independence."

Start Planning Today

Throughout this book we've given you solid advice, reasons, and action tips for creating a comprehensive success map for your real estate career, no matter what stage of the game you're at. Remember that a business plan is not only critical to the success of a new business, but it can also help existing business owners stay on track and hone the future of their business.

And although it is certainly possible to start and run a real estate business without a plan, the chances for success improve greatly when you have a detailed blueprint to follow. Plus, the exercise of creating the plan forces you to think through issues that might otherwise be overlooked, such as:

- ❑ Who are my competitors?
- ❑ How big is my target market?
- ❑ How can I reach this target market?
- ❑ What would happen if I were to expand my farm area by 500 houses?
- ❑ How much business would I lose if I took a two-week vacation?
- ❑ How much cash flow does my business generate?
- ❑ What is my company's profit and loss?
- ❑ What do I need to do to earn an additional $15,000 in commissions each year?
- ❑ How much should I allocate for advertising?
- ❑ How can I find someone to help me serve my growing client base?
- ❑ What kind of marketing works best in my area?
- ❑ How can I minimize my tax obligations?
- ❑ How will I pay for my child's college education?
- ❑ When can I retire?

These and other elements can be incorporated into a comprehensive business plan that puts your career heads and tails above the rest. Many other agents may plod along wondering where their next commission check is going to come from, but you'll already know that answer because you've thought through all of the essentials of running a business. It means much more than just serving as an intermediary for buyers and sellers of homes. Don't fret if you've been doing that all along, as there's no time like the present to take your business off autopilot and shake things up a bit with a few good planning sessions. Good luck!

Sample Business Plans

When developing your business plan, you'll probably fall into one of two camps:

1. You're a new agent who needs a roadmap for success.
2. You're an existing agent (with two or more years of experience in the field) and you either need to develop your first plan or tweak one for maximum effectiveness.

In this section, we'll look at two sample business plans. The first focuses on the new agent who has already hung her license at a broker's office and is working hard to get to that first sale. The second centers on an agent who wants more out of his existing business. Use these sample plans as a guide when creating your own success strategies, but remember there are many variations to business plans, and you'll probably need to tailor the format around your own business.

Sample Business Plan #1: New Agent

SUMMARY

Executive Summary: Rhonda Jones is a new residential real estate agent who passed her licensing exam and hung her license with ABC Realty in the town of Allentown, Pennsylvania. Armed with a limited amount of sales knowledge and several years of experience as an office manager at a small industrial company, Jones has resided in Allentown for fifteen years and has a vast network of friends and family in the region. This real estate agent is technologically savvy, having worked in an office for a number of years. Her knowledge of the real estate industry is limited, although she's very familiar with the communities in which she will be serving as a trusted adviser through the home buying and selling process.

Business Concept: Jones will work with home buyers and sellers in the residential real estate industry. Working on a 50/50 commission split with her broker, Jones will charge the going commission rate of 6 percent for her services, splitting the fee with the cooperating broker. Using a combination of farming, floor time at her broker's office, canvassing of neighborhoods, and various advertising methods, Jones will list homes for sale and work with buyers, helping them find the home of their dreams in exchange for a commission.

Current Situation: Jones has yet to list or sell a home and is currently in the process of networking with her friends and family to get the word out about her new business. Through several hours of floor time, she has shown a few homes in the area to interested new buyers, none of whom made offers on the homes.

Key Success Factors: Jones knows her geographic region like the back of her hand and is able to discuss intelligently the various neighborhoods in that region. She has a large network of potential clients and is technologically savvy enough to make use of valuable tools like the online MLS, electronic lockboxes, personal digital assistants, and the Internet.

Key Challenges: Jones lacks an in-depth knowledge of her

local real estate market in terms of its size, number of existing and new home sales, and related information. She's also just learning how the cooperation between brokers works in the industry.

Financial Situation/Needs: Jones has a six-month cash reserve that she's hoping will see her through the first few lean months in the real estate business. With just a few weeks under her belt, Jones needs to close one or more deals within the next six months in order to sustain herself in her current, full-time position as an agent. She has no dependents and is therefore able to take a slightly higher risk for the next six months to a year without putting anyone (except herself) in financial jeopardy. Jones has a small retirement fund—started at her previous job—which she plans to begin funding again when it's financially feasible. She has also obtained health insurance (via the COBRA system) from her last employer, at her own expense.

VISION

Vision Statement: By acting as a facilitator during the home buying and selling process for citizens in her geographic region, and by providing the highest possible service levels to those individuals, Jones will create a business that supports her lifestyle while also allowing her to save for her future. To make that happen, Jones will continually hone her professional skills through training, earn the appropriate designations, and operate in a fair, ethical manner.

MARKET ANALYSIS

The Overall Market: Through information garnered from the local MLS system and various real estate research companies, Jones knows that the existing home market is brisk in the Lehigh Valley region of Pennsylvania. Homes priced in the $150,000 to $250,000 range tend to sell the fastest. There is also a high demand for more affordable housing (although availability of such homes is scarce at this time).

Changes in the Market: Like most of the United States, the Lehigh Valley area has experienced significant property appreciation rates (of 10 to 15 percent, on average) over the last two years. Although much of the housing stock is fifty-plus years old in the region, there has been an influx of new home construction during that time, based on job growth at many of the region's larger manufacturers and distribution facilities.

Target Market and Customers: With her office situated in the city of Allentown, Jones has chosen to focus her efforts on the city itself, plus nearby suburban areas like Bath, Trexlertown, Macungie, and other largely residential communities. Her target customers include first-time home buyers, relocating professionals (based on her company's national referral database), and individuals and families who are "moving up" into larger homes. Because Jones is single, she will also target the growing legion of single home buyers, with whom she can relate and help guide through the home buying process.

COMPETITIVE ANALYSIS

Industry Overview: The Lehigh Valley real estate market is competitive, but not to the point where there isn't any room for a new agent in the mix. The industry comprises full-service brokerages to discount brokers, and everything in between. Full-service agents tend to dominate the marketplace, as they have for years, with names like Coldwell Banker and Century 21 dotting the landscape and claiming the bulk of the market share.

Nature of Competition: Although full-service companies hold most of the cards in Jones's marketplace, there has been some erosion not only from discount brokers, but also from those sellers who choose to go it alone with the help of a real estate agent. Competition for listings is tight, so working with buyers can be a good way to create business, since relocations to large companies like Air Products and Chemicals Inc. are fairly regular.

Competitors: Key competitors in the market include agents who work for other full-service companies, discount and flat-fee brokerages, and do-it-yourself shops. Competitors also include those home sellers who opt for the For Sale By Owner (FSBO) route.

Opportunities: For new agents who are willing to put their noses to the grindstone by farming, advertising, and networking, there are significant opportunities both in Allentown and in the surrounding communities. Situated within driving distance of New York City and Philadelphia, for example, the area has attracted a number of residents who commute to such cities daily, but who opt to live in a more rural environment. There are also several large colleges in the region (Muhlenberg and Lehigh University, for example) that attract students who wind up staying there after graduation.

STRATEGY

Key Competitive Capabilities: Jones is very familiar with the market itself and knows the characteristics of the various neighborhoods, schools, and other important considerations. She also has a significant network of friends, family, and colleagues who will either work with her when buying or selling a home, or point other customers in her direction.

An affable individual, Jones has the right personality for a real estate agent.

Key Competitive Weaknesses: Jones has never owned her own business, and as such does not know what it really takes to be a real estate agent. She also lacks knowledge of the real estate industry itself and is unaware of exactly how commission structures, contracts, inspections, and other related issues work.

Strategy: By selecting a broker that offers extensive training, Jones has set herself up to learn about the real estate industry before having to jump in feetfirst. She'll spend the first few months in the industry either in training or working with an experienced agent to learn about contracts, inspections, and other important issues. Jones will also enroll in her local college's SBDC and take several introduction to business courses to learn the basics of running a small business.

MARKETING AND SALES

Marketing Strategy: Jones's initial marketing efforts will be directed at her own sphere of influence—or those people to whom she's already connected. She'll add to that stable of potential clients by doing several hours of floor time at the broker's office. Jones will select a farm area of about 500 homes as a starting point, then increase that area as she gains experience in the industry. Her broker will assign her the farm area, based on where she lives and how well she knows the neighborhood in question.

Sales Tactics: Using direct mail, door-to-door, and cold calling (when allowed by state and federal do-not-call laws), Jones will target her farm area from various angles with "Just Listed" and "Just Sold" postcards, as well as general, introductory-type postcards. Jones will also pay attention to expired listings and FSBOs in her target areas. She will approach them with a clear, crisp sales message based on her own merits, as well as those of her brokerage, which has been operating in the region for over thirty years.

Advertising: Jones's early print advertising efforts will be limited, but will increase as she lists homes for sale. She will make good use of the Internet, as her broker allows individual agents to set up their own Web sites. Through pay-per-click advertising online, Jones will invest a small amount of money to drive traffic to her Web site. She will also investigate the various online lead-generation Web sites to find out if that investment will be worthwhile as a new agent.

Promotions and Publicity: Taking advantage of local media opportunities, Jones will first ask her broker to announce her addition to the team in the local newspaper. From there, she will keep an eye out for opportunities to sponsor events, volunteer her time to local service groups, and thus create other newsworthy happenings that can help get her name out into the public eye.

DOLLARS AND CENTS

The Financials: Jones has six months' worth of cash reserves, and as such will need to close her first sale within that time period, or preferably sooner. Working backward, she'll need to get either a listing or a solid buyer within the next sixty days, then attempt to close the deal within the following 120 days. Jones has a retirement account that she can tap, if needed, but her ultimate goal is to be at the closing table to receive a commission check within her first six months in business.

Financial Assistance: To make sure that she's adequately

planning not only for the immediate future but also for the long-term, Jones will sit down with an accountant early in the game to set up a good record-keeping system, do tax planning, and figure out some key projections for her new company. When the time is right, Jones will also begin investing in her retirement again, purchase a health insurance plan on her own (or through a group like the National Association of Realtors), and take other steps to prepare for her future.

Keeping Records: To track her income and expenses, Jones will use a Microsoft Excel spreadsheet to itemize income sources as well as business and personal expenses. She'll use a balance sheet and keep updated cash flow and profit and loss projections in order to see exactly where she stands at any given time. Jones will use this information when making strategic business decisions.

Sample Business Plan #2: Existing Agent

SUMMARY

Executive Summary: Alex Chavez is a residential real estate agent who has been working in the field for just over two years. He is a full-service agent who works on a typical commission rate of 6 percent, split with the cooperating broker on each deal. Because he works for a 100-percent brokerage, Chavez does not split his side of the commission with his broker, but instead pays a monthly, flat fee to use the broker's physical location and related services. Based in Coral Gables, Florida, Chavez has extensive knowledge of his surrounding community. An entrepreneur by nature, Chavez also has good business acumen and a handle on the financial aspect of running a real estate business, but he's dissatisfied with his results over the last year. Chavez is ready to take his business to the next level.

Business Concept: Chavez is an ABR who works solely with home buyers. Chavez charges the going commission rate of 6 percent for his services and retains all of his commissions on a 100-percent basis. He gets the majority of his business through personal contacts, the company's nationwide referral system, and Internet lead-generation services like Home Gain.com and HouseHunt.com. Chavez handles the buy side of the deal, helping buyers find the homes of their dreams, negotiating on their behalf, coordinating inspections and disclosures, and providing the buyer with professional advice and guidance in finding the right property at the right price.

Current Situation: Chavez has closed seventeen deals during his two years in the business, for a total of $127,000 in gross commissions. He's now ready to ramp up and do a higher volume of business.

Key Success Factors: Chavez is very familiar with his geographic region and can discuss intelligently the various neighborhoods in that area. He has a large network of potential clients and is technologically savvy enough to make use of valuable tools like the online MLS, electronic lockboxes, personal digital assistants, and the Internet. Chavez is fluent in Spanish and is able to communicate effectively with the Latino home buyers in his region.

Key Challenges: Chavez jumped into real estate and experienced early success, but never took the time to create a solid business and marketing plan. As such, he's been working hard with buyers but lives deal-to-deal and is unable to predict profits and losses, cash flow, and other important business concepts. The day-to-day tasks keep him busy, but he knows he could be working more efficiently if he were to take the time to create projections and revamp his marketing and advertising efforts.

Financial Situation/Needs: Chavez is married with one child. His spouse earns about $40,000 annually and is able to pay all household bills on that income. She also has health insurance and is investing in a retirement plan. Chavez earned $30,000 during his first year in real estate and $97,000 during the second year.

VISION

Vision Statement: By acting as a facilitator during the home buying process for citizens in his geographic region, and by providing the highest possible service levels to those individuals, Chavez has created a business that supports his lifestyle and allows him to save for the future. By focusing solely on buyers, Chavez is able to channel his energy into a specific aspect of the real estate industry and has become well known for his abilities in this area.

MARKET ANALYSIS

The Overall Market: Through information garnered from the local MLS system and various real estate research companies, Chavez knows that the existing home market is hot in southern Florida, where homes priced below $200,000 are in big demand, yet very hard to come by. Homes priced in the $250,000 to $400,000 range sell best, with higher-end homes also in demand in the region.

Changes in the Market: Like most of the United States, southern Florida has experienced significant property appreciation rates (of 15 to 25 percent, on average) over the last two years. An influx of new construction can't keep pace with demand, making it a definite seller's market at this time. The region attracts a great deal of international second-home buyers, as well as relocating professionals, retirees, and those looking for vacation homes in warm climates.

Target Market and Customers: With his office situated in the upscale city of Coral Gables, Chavez helps buyers find homes within the city and in outlying, residential areas. His target customers are often second-home buyers or relocating professionals who use Internet search tools like Realtor .com to search for homes. Chavez also works with some first-time home buyers from the Hispanic community and international buyers from Latin America but has yet to fully tap either one of these markets.

COMPETITIVE ANALYSIS

Industry Overview: The southern Florida real estate market is extremely competitive, but Chavez has managed to carve out a place for himself by working with a broad range of potential buyers. The landscape comprises full-service brokerages to discount brokers, and everything in between. No one type of real estate company dominates the marketplace.

Nature of Competition: Market-share erosion by discount, Internet, and flat-fee brokers runs rampant in southern Florida. Competition for listings is tight, which makes buyer representation a popular choice among agents. However, the lack of inventory (particularly in the most desirable price ranges) means buyer's agents like Chavez are forced to deal with multiple offers, strict time frames, and inspection waiving in order to connect the right buyer with the right home.

Competitors: Key competitors in the market include agents who work for other full-service companies, discount and flat-fee brokerages, and do-it-yourself shops. Competitors also include those home sellers who opt for the For Sale By Owner (FSBO) route.

Opportunities: There are many opportunities for Spanish-speaking real estate agents who truly know the market and can negotiate on the buyer's behalf. There is also a significant opportunity in southern Florida within the international buyer marketplace, and among the nation's largest-growing group of home buyers: the U.S. Hispanic population.

STRATEGY

Key Competitive Capabilities: Chavez is very familiar with the market itself and knows the characteristics of the various neighborhoods, schools, and other important considerations. During his first two years in the industry, he received much training and mentoring on the business itself, and is well equipped to run a successful real estate practice.

Key Competitive Weaknesses: Because he never took the time to create a plan of attack, Chavez is missing out on several key market segments, namely international buyers and Hispanic home buyers. Both could benefit greatly from his expertise and honest, ethical business practices. Caught up in the day-to-day aspects of running his business and dealing mainly with referrals and leads generated online, this buyer's agent needs to hone his strategy to maximize those key market segments.

Strategy: Chavez will revamp his marketing strategy to target those two groups of potential buyers while also scaling up his own business to accommodate the increase. This can be accomplished by pairing up with another agent whose skills complement his, hiring a full-time, part-time, or virtual assistant, or forming a team, as many 100-percent agents do when they reach a certain level of success.

MARKETING AND SALES

Marketing Strategy: Chavez has largely relied on traditional referral, Internet referral, and word of mouth to bring business to his door. In order to get to the next level, he'll need to expand those marketing efforts to include a few appropriate niches that fit well with his own business style and personal experience.

Sales Tactics: Using targeted advertising in magazines that overseas buyers will be likely to read, Web sites that appeal to international and Latino home buyers, and print ads that reach out to such customers, Chavez will attract more potential customers while continuing to work his existing sales channels to create a well-rounded sales strategy.

Advertising: Armed with a small advertising budget, Chavez will create Spanish- and English-language advertising for targeted media outlets (such as local Spanish-language newspapers in southern Florida) that appeals to (1) first-time Hispanic home buyers who need an experienced, bilingual agent who can educate them and help them navigate the complex process; and (2) international buyers from places like Latin America, where wealthy individuals are eager to put their money in the U.S. housing market.

Promotions and Publicity: Chavez will maximize his position as a successful Hispanic businessperson in southern Florida by participating in events and volunteering several hours a month to community causes that reach out to a specific demographic: Hispanic families that are renting and would benefit from purchasing a home but don't know how to go about it. He will also consider teaching a quarterly home buying course at a local venue. Although he can't directly solicit customers through the course, they will remember him and have his literature on hand for quick reference when they are ready to buy a home.

DOLLARS AND CENTS

The Financials: Chavez is one of those lucky agents who has ample time to build his business while his significant other handles much of the household financial burden. This will allow Chavez to channel some of his profits back into technology, Internet expenses, and advertising as he ramps up his business. He will also be able to afford either to hire a part-time assistant to handle much of the day-to-day (nontransaction-related) tasks, or to contract some of that work to a virtual assistant.

Financial Assistance: Now that his business is in growth mode, Chavez will sit down with an accountant and/or financial planner to decide whether it's time to incorporate his business and set up a retirement account in order to sock away pretax dollars for his future. Chavez will also enlist the accountant's help in creating a more formal bookkeeping system, a plan for tax payments, and a quick and easy tracking system for his business's profits and losses.

Keeping Records: To track income and expenses, Chavez will use a Microsoft Excel spreadsheet to itemize income sources as well as to list business and personal expenditures. Utilizing a balance sheet, he'll keep updated cash flow and profit and loss projections to see exactly where he stands at any given time. Chavez will use this information when making strategic business decisions.

Business Plan Outline

Business plans come in all shapes and sizes, and are generally tailored to the specific company or type of business that you're starting or expanding. Here's a general outline to use when creating your own business plan.

1. *Cover Sheet:* This page should reflect the image of your new company and include any logos or graphics that you plan to use during the course of business. Use "Business Plan for _____" as the title, and be sure to date the plan.

_____
_____
_____
_____
_____
_____
_____
_____
_____
_____

2. *Table of Contents:* List each section and subsection throughout the plan.

_____
_____
_____
_____
_____
_____
_____
_____
_____

3. *Executive Summary:* A one- to two-page summary of your business plan. Summarize the key points covered in the plan, and include a complete-but-brief overview of your plan.

_____
_____
_____
_____
_____
_____
_____

4. *Industry/Market Analysis:* An overview of your industry and the market you'll be targeting.

_____
_____
_____
_____
_____
_____
_____

5. *Business Overview:* A description of the products or services you'll be selling, how long your company has been in operation, and a few short-term and long-term business goals.

_____
_____
_____
_____
_____
_____
_____

6. *Ownership and Legal Structure:* A snapshot of the company's ownership structure and choice of business entity (corporation, sole proprietorship, etc.)

_____
_____
_____
_____
_____
_____
_____

7. *Management and Staffing:* Describe the roles that current or future team members or employees will fill in your growing business, and detail your plans for adding human resources to your operation as it grows and prospers.

_____

_____

_____

_____

_____

8. *Marketing Plan:* A thorough look at how you will market or sell your services to your customers.

_____

_____

_____

_____

_____

9. *Financial Plan:* An honest assessment of how much money you'll need to get this business off the ground and just how that money will be used, including a valid reason for those expenditures.

_____

_____

_____

_____

_____

_____

10. *Business Strengths and Weaknesses:* Your company's strongest points, and where it needs more work in order to grow and thrive in the marketplace.

_____

_____

_____

_____

_____

_____

11. *Growth Projections:* Exactly how you want (and expect) your company to grow over the next several months, with longer-term projections that include the next two to five years.

_____

_____

_____

_____

_____

_____

_____

12. *Exit Strategy:* A detailed look at how you would plan to sell or otherwise leave the business, when the time comes to do so.

_____

_____

_____

_____

_____

_____

Business Planning Resources for Real Estate Agents

Online Planning Resources

BizPlanIt.com
www.bizplanit.com
A consulting company offering customized business plan development services.

Entrepreneur magazine
www.entrepreneur.com
Site includes a wide variety of articles on starting, managing, and growing a business, including in-depth information on business planning.

NEBS
www.nebs.com/NASApp/nebsEcat/business_tools/bptemplate/index.jsp
A business plan template that you can use to develop your own business plan.

SCORE
www.score.org
Site includes a wide variety of articles and information about business planning and related topics.

The Small Business Administration
www.sba.gov/index.html
Includes many different resources for small-business owners who need information on basic business planning, financing, and related issues.

Books

Covello, Joseph A., and Brian Hazelgren. *Your First Business Plan: A Simple Question and Answer Format Designed to Help You Write Your Own Plan.* Naperville, Illinois: Sourcebooks, Inc., 1998.

Hargrave, Lee E. *Plan for Profitability: How to Write a Strategic Business Plan.* Titusville, Florida: Four Seasons Publishers, 1999.

O'Donnell, Michael. *Writing Business Plans That Get Results: A Step-By-Step Guide.* Chicago: Contemporary Books, 1991.

Tiffany, Paul, and Steven Peterson. *Business Plans for Dummies.* Foster City, California: IDG Books, 1997.

Software

BPlans Software
www.bplans.com
On this site you can access information about business-planning software and read articles on basic and advanced business planning.

Business Plan Pro

www.paloalto.com/ps/bp/
A software program that offers over 400 sample business plans, an EasyPlan Wizard, and easy-to-use tables.

Plan Magic

http://planmagic.com/
Features an easy-to-use browser interface for the guide, product-line analysis, detailed marketing concept, financial workbook, and automated charts.

Plan-Write

www.brs-inc.com
Available in several versions, includes a library of sample business plans, a business-plan wizard, and step-by-step instructions.

Index